Anders Boulanger is, without a doubt, <del>the most</del> *engaging* people I know — both personally <del>and professionally.</del> Few people understand, let alone have mastered, the skill to create immediate, impactful, and unforgettable connection through engagement like Anders has. The good news (for all of us!) is he articulately and generously shares how he does it and how you can benefit from greater engagement in all aspects of your life with *Engage First.*

Rob Wozny, SCMP,
Author, *Storytelling for Business: The art & science of creating connection in the digital age*

Engage First by Anders Boulanger is a timely exploration of how authentic human connection is being lost in an age of constant connectivity. In a world where social media and digital noise often isolate more than unite, Boulanger offers a powerful call to reclaim meaningful engagement. Through sharp insights and actionable strategies, he challenges readers to break free from their bubbles, communicate with purpose, and lead with presence in both business and life.

Scott Lillis,
President & CEO of The Lillis Technology Group

Engage First is a must-read for anyone looking to stand out and make every interaction matter. Anders Boulanger combines performance art with the science of human connection to create a practical guide for capturing attention and building trust in our busy world. Through engaging stories and useful strategies, this book explains why engagement is important and shows you how to achieve it, whether you're leading a team, selling a product, or simply wanting to improve your relationships.

What makes this book special is its hands-on approach. Each chapter is packed with real-life examples, memorable stories, and practical exercises that make the ideas easy to apply. Boulanger's genuine and warm writing makes complex ideas simple and encourages readers to step out of their comfort zones. If you want to be more impactful and memorable in every conversation, *Engage First* will give you the tools and confidence to do just that.

Jim Tedesco,
General Manager and SVP Customer Success,
Veeam Software

Engage First is a practical, inspiring guide to mastering the art of human connection. Anders Boulanger blends storytelling, psychology, and real-world experience to show you how to stand out, build trust, and make every interaction count. Whether you're in sales, leadership, or public speaking, this book gives you the tools to truly engage. A must-read in today's distracted world!

Deri Latimer,
Speaker, Author, *Resilience Rebel*

ENGAGE FIRST

Capture Attention, Build Trust, and Drive Real Results

ANDERS BOULANGER

First published in Great Britain by Practical Inspiration Publishing, 2025

ISBN   9781788608398 (hardback)
        9781788608404 (paperback)
        9781788608411 (ebook)

EU GPSR representative: LOGOS EUROPE, 9 rue Nicolas Poussin, LA ROCHELLE 17000, France Contact@logoseurope.eu

Want to bulk-buy copies of this book for your team and colleagues? We can customize the content and co-brand *Engage First* to suit your business's needs.

Please email info@practicalinspiration.com for more details.

Practical Inspiration Publishing

To my wife, Robbyn — for being my greatest supporter, my early proofreader, and my constant sounding board throughout this journey.

To my amazing kids, Keaton and Esmee — thank you for your love, laughter, and for being the best kids a dad could ask for.

And to Boyd Liski, my longtime Chief Strategy Officer — for keeping me focused and holding me accountable to finish what I started.

Contents

Foreword

Shep Hyken

Customer service & experience expert and *New York Times* bestselling author.

Engagement is everything. In business, in customer service, and in life, engagement is the foundation upon which relationships are built. Whether you're trying to earn a sale, create a memorable customer experience, or simply hold someone's attention, engagement is the currency that fuels meaningful interactions. And that's exactly why this book, *Engage First*, is so important.

When I first started studying customer service and experience, I quickly realized that businesses that won customers—and kept them—were the ones that understood that every interaction counts. They weren't just delivering a product or a service; they were creating a positive connection. They understood that before you can influence, persuade, or sell, you have to engage. This is a principle that holds true in every industry, from retail to B2B sales, from hospitality to technology. Engagement isn't a nice-to-have; it's the foundation of success.

This book goes deep into the art and science of engagement. It isn't just about getting people to listen—it's about making sure they care. It's about standing out in a world that is saturated with distractions. Let's face it: we live in an era where attention spans are shrinking, and consumers have more choices than ever before. If you don't grab someone's attention and hold it, you've lost them. That's why engagement isn't just a buzzword—it's a survival strategy.

The principles in *Engage First* align closely with what I've been teaching for years about customer service and experience. The best companies—the ones that earn repeat business and build strong relationships—understand that engagement is an ongoing process. It starts with that initial moment of connection, but it continues with every interaction. Whether you're talking to a customer at a trade show, presenting a new idea to your team, or handling a customer service issue, engagement is what turns ordinary moments into extraordinary ones.

What makes this book particularly valuable is its focus on actionable strategies. It doesn't just tell you why engagement matters—it shows you how to make it happen. From understanding the psychology of attention to mastering the skills of compelling storytelling, this book provides a roadmap for anyone who wants to be more engaging in their work and in their interactions.

One of the concepts I talk about often is "creating *Moments of Magic*®." These are the moments where a business goes above and beyond to surprise and delight a customer. But here's the thing—those moments don't happen by accident. They happen because someone made an intentional effort to engage first. When you create a moment of engagement, you create an opportunity to build trust, spark interest, and leave a lasting impression.

Anders Boulanger understands this better than most. He's spent his career perfecting the art of engagement, whether it's on stage, at a trade show, or in everyday conversations. His insights are powerful because they're rooted in real-world experience. He doesn't just talk about engagement—he lives it. And that's why this book is so valuable. It's not a collection of theories; it's a playbook that's been tested in the field.

If you're a business leader, a salesperson, a speaker, or anyone who wants to connect more effectively with people, you need this book.

Engagement is what makes the difference between being heard and being remembered. It's what separates the brands that people love from the ones they forget. And it's what will help you build stronger relationships, close more deals, and create experiences that truly matter.

So, as you dive into the pages of *Engage First*, get ready to rethink the way you communicate. Get ready to sharpen your ability to capture and hold attention. Most importantly, get ready to engage first—and watch what happens when you do.

Introduction

Most people don't read the introduction of a book. They want to get right to the heart of the content as fast as possible. This is also true with many of our personal interactions in real life. We are in such a hurry to get to the point of why we are there—we don't take the time to build rapport, connect, and engage with the person in front of us.

If you picked up this book, I'm going to go out on a limb and say you are looking to get a greater return on your interactions. You want people to listen to you, remember what you said and act on that conversation.

Many of us can feel ignored or even invisible in today's world.

We tend to ignore the supermarket cashier; we maybe give a cursory smile or perfunctory hello. Conversation is kept to a minimum and we go about our day. In many cases we didn't even see a cashier, instead we used the self-checkout and didn't have to engage with anyone during our visit. We missed out on the experience of interacting with others and therefore no engagement skills were needed, let alone developed and honed.

I wrote this book to help combat some of the engagement issues that are taking place in society. Every day our attention is being hijacked by the technological distractions around us. Our focus is fragmented thanks to ads and deceptive online articles that try and get us to click and go down yet another rabbit hole of distractions. Not to mention our phone with its incessant notifications buzzing and beeping all hours of the day, vying for our focus.

So, two things are happening simultaneously. We call this the engagement gap. We as humans engage with each other less because of fewer necessary interactions in our daily lives. In many areas, technology has eliminated the need to engage with others (banking, shopping, working from home, etc.). So, we are not in the habit of being proactive and engaging with people. Our engagement muscles are anemic. In short, we are losing our ability to connect and engage with one another.

The other side of the engagement gap is that we tend to avoid being engaged with in the first place. In an attempt to control the incoming stimuli, we shy away from getting involved. The increased demands on our attention and time have given rise to thinking less of the value of each interaction. We quickly dismiss the calls for our attention and treat every attempt as a telemarketer vying for just a minute of your time.

While it's a good thing to guard our time, attention, and wallet, we run the risk of throwing the baby out with the bathwater. We shut down valid attempts of others to create connection.

By avoiding the incoming engagement, we are shutting ourselves down to many possibilities that we'll never know. Fewer friends that we'll meet, sales we'll never make and new adventures that will never be had.

When we engage with others, it opens a door that leads to a series of additional doors. These potential outcomes are only possible if the person you interact with is paying attention, cares about you and cares about the conversation.

Picture a hotel conference room full of people attempting to watch the dryest, most boring keynote on technology they've ever seen. At the end of the hour the crowd slowly files out of the room, having lost 60 minutes of their life that they'll never get back.

Two days later, they sadly only remember 10% of the content and can't even remember the name of the presenter or the company that speaker represented. If the speaker was bad, it might not be surprising to learn that the speaker wasn't paid to be there. It might, however, surprise you that the speaker slot was paid for by his company, and it cost a whopping $60,000!

This is not some hypothetical situation; this happens at conferences around the world every day! While companies may talk themselves into believing it's worth it, I'd beg to differ. This speaker not only wasted his own time but his audience's collective time and even squandered the $60k investment. This is an example of the real-world costs of not engaging first.

If you want to learn to communicate more effectively, connect with people more deeply and persuade others to your way of thinking, you must start by engaging first. Without capturing the attention of your counterpart, your time, effort, and money will be wasted.

In Part 1 of this book, we'll look at why you'd want to learn to engage first. We'll go deeper into the causes of what's creating the engagement gap and motivate you to do and be more in your interactions.

In Part 2, we'll explore the basics of being engaging and how we can use these fundamentals to up our connection in face-to-face situations.

Last, we'll explore more advanced techniques that will require more work and dedication to master. While these concepts require more focus and practice, they are more than worth the effort required.

Where applicable, I've included some engagement challenges for you to try to allow you to develop the skill sets discussed in each chapter.

If you stuck with me through this introduction, if I was able to engage your mind sufficiently, I hope that you find yourself primed to dig into the contents of this book.

My goal for you as a reader is to better understand this engagement gap and learn the skills, tactics, and techniques taught here so that you can get more of what you want out of every interaction.

PART 1
WHY ENGAGE FIRST?

Chapter 1
The state of engagement

Every year in late January or early February, the President of the United States delivers the State of the Union Address. This formal affair is a means to underline the current condition of the nation. Everything from the economy to upcoming priorities for the administration are covered. In this chapter, I will lay out the current "State of Engagement," how I've seen things change over time, and what we can potentially do about this deterioration.

Over my lifetime, audience behavior has shifted. People are not as easy to please as they once were. Having made my living by entertaining people for the last 25 years, I've seen the attention spans of audience members plummet. What used to entertain and delight them, now doesn't seem to cut it. For a quick example, go on YouTube and watch some of the contestants from the first season of *America's Got Talent*. What used to seem amazing can seem commonplace today.

Younger generations have had more exposure at an earlier age to more engaging content. Perhaps you've heard your parents or grandparents talk about how they seemed to entertain themselves with nothing but a ball and a stick. By contrast, how many toddlers in strollers do you see with a tablet or phone in their hand?

The rise of the smartphone plays a large role in the level of distraction and stimulation we endure on a daily basis. Our connectedness to the digital world has disconnected us from the personal world. We carry around with us a pocket full of buzzing, beeping, notifying distractions that keep us up to date but down the rabbit hole of our own personal digital bubble.

When instant messenger applications and chat groups were new, the acronym BRB was coined to indicate that you were still around but momentarily away from your keyboard. You'd "Be Right Back." These days, BRB is no longer in the texting lexicon. We are rarely away from our phones and the ability to communicate. We assume that everyone is always available, waiting with bated breath to respond to us. If they have their phones nearby, they are fair game. Added to this is the deluge of app notifications that demand our attention every waking minute.

The following picture shows a crowd at a vendor's booth at a trade show in Las Vegas in 2018. I was fascinated by the sight of the crowd, many of them detached from their environment.

Upon closer examination, you'll notice that only four people are actively paying any attention to the presenter. The rest are tuned out—heads down and shut down, on their phones and in their own little worlds or chatting among themselves. This lack of attention isn't just happening at trade shows either—this is the default setting in which most people function daily. We are detached by default. It takes something compelling to shake us from our preoccupation.

In today's world, to create engagement we must do more than we have in the past. We must compete in the world of distractions and out-engage the pull of the digital world. We need to create moments of pure personal interaction that transcend our usual day-to-day existence. To be noticed and stand out, we must do what others aren't willing to do.

We need to get people heads-up and lit-up. We need to give them a strong reason to be a part of an interaction so that they're more interested in what we have to offer than what their dopamine-spiking device will deliver. Creating engagement means that your audience is ready and willing to consume whatever is being offered. That's the goal—to have the kind of buy-in where energy is freely exchanged without restriction.

I like to perform in close proximity to my audience. The nearer a presenter is to their audience, the more they demand to be seen, and the bigger the presenter is in the field of vision.

Believe it or not, even with a short distance between us, I sometimes still catch people on their phones. Just like a teacher, I'll scold them (tongue-in-cheek, of course, so as not to lose rapport with the crowd), and sometimes if they're close enough, I'll grab the phone out of their hands.

With phone in hand, I hold it up and say, "These devices are designed to connect us to the rest of the world, and yet they disconnect us from the best of the world—what's right here in front of you. It takes you out of the present and makes you absent. You know what's better than 8K, 3D, Retina display? Looking at life through your own eyes. I've spent my life honing my skills preparing for this very moment for you to be here with me right now. With that being said, raise your hand if you'd like to have a true experience." I then hand back the phone and continue with my presentation. My little soapbox speech gets everyone in line for the rest of the performance.

No doubt you've heard phones ringing in a theater during a show, or seen people who are so focused on catching everything through their viewfinders that they fail to live an experience through their own eyes. Mobile device distraction is so prevalent, I've heard cases of it detracting from the arts; restaurant magicians report that while performing a second trick for a table of people, some people in the group will be heads down on their phones, trying to look up how the first trick was done. We are drowning in information, yet missing out on the experiences right in front of us.

Data dump

It's no wonder that engagement is waning in our society. We are pelted with as much data in a day as someone from the 15th century would see in an entire lifetime. In the span of one minute, 16 million text messages are sent throughout the world, 208,000 pictures are uploaded to Facebook, and 2.4 million search requests are fielded on Google.

We have access to as much content as we could possibly want. As a kid, I had three channels of TV available, so it was easy to pick the best thing on at any given time and watch it. Now the problem isn't finding something good to watch, it's choosing *which* good thing to watch. My wife and I can spend 30 minutes just deciding on which show to choose!

This overwhelm creates disengagement. People tune out when it just becomes *too much*. They choose to sit on the sidelines rather than trying to make sense of the confusion. Our bodies are made for survival and our brain requires a great deal of energy. Rather than burning valuable calories trying to make sense of the confusion, our brain tunes out complexity as a means of self-preservation.

Unfortunately, this overwhelm problem isn't going to go away. The world isn't getting simpler, it's getting more complex by the day. This means that learning to engage will only become more important in the future as we attempt to communicate with audiences in various states of overwhelm.

Deluge of distractions

Very closely related to data are the notifications of the data. We are bombarded by tiny digital taps on the shoulder that tear our attention away from what we are doing. Each ping and banner hinting at a potential affirmation or signaling love for a social media post gives us a dopamine hit. Just like a bite of something sweet, this dopamine spike trains us to look at our phones and check them, taking us out of the current moment.

When you hear the ping of a notification, it creates an open loop that demands to be closed. We can't stand the "not knowing," and it becomes an itch that we want to scratch. Technology is competing for our attention alongside the normal demands of daily life. Today, working from home has also become more common, which only adds to the distractions people face in a workday. Dealing with emails, deadlines, and virtual meetings may now be accompanied by a dog barking, a baby crying, or the sound of a spouse on a Zoom call.

Not only are you and I distracted, so is everyone around us. Have you ever had a conversation with someone who seems to be looking over your shoulder or is constantly checking their phone? This is becoming the norm and we need to learn how to thrive in this new world.

Signal versus noise

So here we are—getting bombarded with data, distracted by interruptions—and the worst part is that much of the noise is exactly that... noise. It's not relevant to anything in our daily lives. We put up with it and train ourselves to tune most of it out because so little of it truly affects us.

When I first started performing trade show magic for companies, the concept of having entertainment alone was enough to entice attendees to stop and watch. Yet because entertainment in and of itself isn't necessarily relevant to business at large industry trade shows, it could easily be ignored. I found that being *relevant* to the conference and the attendees was integral to the overall engagement impact a presentation could have. Adding a marketing message and making the magic trick answer a particular problem made the presentation more salient.

The state of engagement in the world today is such that people are willfully ignoring attempts at connection because they assume that the interaction can't possibly benefit them. Just think of all the junk phone calls you get in a day. When you look at the call display some of the numbers are so long and strange looking we know they can't possibly be from someone we know or want to hear from—and we don't even bother answering. If people pre-judge what comes at them as noise instead of a signal to pay attention, they become very difficult to engage.

Path of least resistance

We now have multiple options available to us for communication. In the distant past, we could only send letters and speak in person. Thanks to Alexander Graham Bell, the telephone was invented, so real-time audio conversations could take place. Today we have texting, direct messaging via social media, video calls, and everybody's favorite: email. Humans are inherently lazy by nature. If there is a shortcut or an easy way out, we'll be sure to take it. With so many options available, we're free to choose the one that's the most convenient; yet the most convenient medium is rarely the most effective or the most engaging choice available.

This drive for convenience affects both our personal and business interactions. I have often watched my wife exchange countless text messages with her mother—trying to organize plans or get to the bottom of some family drama—when one short phone call would be more to the point and far less frustrating. I know many salespeople who would much rather send an email than pick up the phone to address a problem and talk directly to the customer. Taking the path of least resistance minimizes our ability to engage with others, which compounds the problem. It's as if no one is trying to really connect with anyone anymore.

I see this happen day in and day out on the trade show floor—booth staff who are paid to be "working" a booth but instead are looking at their phones, talking with each other, and generally ignoring the duties they were sent there to do. But even if you don't frequent trade shows, you don't have to look far to find bad customer service resulting from an unwillingness to engage. Just today, I was on my internet service provider's website looking for a number to call. The website instructed me to fill out a form to receive a call back; I did this, expecting to get a phone call, but got another email instead. I replied to this email by giving my cell number and requesting a call back so I could discuss upgrading my internet. This prompted a second email from the internet company. I replied back, repeating my request for a phone call from a service rep to have my questions answered. Nobody ever called me back.

I'm trying to give this company more money per month, and they don't seem to want to take it.

The good news

The good news for us is that the bar is set low. Very low. Ever notice how impressed you are when a store employee is attentive to your needs, or even just polite? Applying the techniques and principles in this book will give you the ability to go above and beyond the current expectation levels of the public and your customers. What used to be ordinary can now be used to your advantage and be extraordinary.

Picking up this book and getting this far means you have a huge opportunity in front of you. Knowing how to be engaging and being willing to make the effort to connect with others will set you apart from 90% of your competition.

Here are four easy ways to go against the grain and up your engagement prowess.

1. Increase the potential level of engagement

Whether that means picking up the phone when you feel like emailing or texting, or meeting through a virtual call instead of the phone, go out of your way to escalate the medium to a more engaging mode of communication. A face-to-face interaction is best, followed by a virtual one, then a phone call, and then text and email. With greater engagement, building relationships, influencing others, and getting your job done more effectively becomes a lot easier.

2. Make the effort

Each time I make a virtual call, I curate my background specifically for that call. For a more professional effect, I close the curtains behind me, turn off one set of lights, and turn on my colored par can lights that illuminate my back wall. I raise my standing desk so I can stand during the call and be more expressive with my body language. All of this takes only a few minutes but makes a world of difference. One client admitted to me that one day, as we met in a virtual call with other marketing professionals, she was multi-tasking on three screens and barely paying attention. But she noticed my lit background, which was quite different from most virtual calls. She leaned in and started to watch and listen more carefully. We won her business that day and she told me it was because of the background lighting that she took a closer look. *To see a video of exactly what I did, go to: https://engagify.ai/a-few-moments-a-world-of-difference/.*

Take the time to do things right. In sales, it takes eight call attempts just to connect with someone on the phone—and thanks to the reasons stated in this chapter, that number is going to increase in coming years. But these increasing barriers to connection doesn't mean we should stop trying.

3. Lead by example

There is a famous saying, "Be the change you want to see in others." If you want the focus on you, give your undivided attention to them. Put your phone away and don't let the distractions of life throw you off. Stop multi-tasking when you are with others. Your presence and connection will rub off on your audience.

Being in the moment is a very rare thing today. That alone can make you stand out. At the very least, you'll make the other person feel acknowledged and heard, which goes a long way towards cementing the relationship.

4. Be relevant

Ensure that your message serves your audience. When your interactions are laced with information that is beneficial to the recipient, those you connect with can't help but listen and pay attention to what you have to offer. (Later in the book, we will devote a full chapter to this idea.)

The bottom line? Be the signal, not the noise.

Chapter 2
The competition
for attention

The number one commodity in marketing is your prospect's attention. Competition for attention in business is fierce.

A great example of this can be seen on any major trade show floor—and I've seen my share of trade shows over the years. I've made my living working as a trade show "infotainer." What is an infotainer, you ask? *Infotainer* is a word we coined to best encapsulate the combination of entertainment and information that we deliver. We mix entertaining skills (usually magic or mentalism) with a company's core marketing message. The result is a high-engagement presentation that stops attendees in the aisles and generates valuable sales leads.

In my time working trade shows, I've seen a myriad of attempts to capture attention and invite attendees to spend more time in a booth. Some approaches are more effective than others. Caricature artists, massage therapists, an American ninja warrior style obstacle course, an escape room—the list goes on and on. Each of them offers a different unique experience that attendees can watch and take part in.

The competition for attention is everywhere. One of the most pervasive and persuasive of these competitors is likely in your pocket, your purse, or even your hand.

In 2020, the documentary *The Social Dilemma* was released on Netflix. It's a fascinating and often disturbing film highlighting the addictive design features that many of today's social media platforms have employed to grow engagement, revenue, and users. In a series of confessions, former engineers and managers at social media companies admit to the use of devious tactics to get us addicted to our phones and their platforms.

One of the former Facebook executives compared what Facebook did to how the tobacco industry evolved their products by adding more nicotine, resulting in increased cravings and sales. In the tech world, this method, known as *growth hacking*, creates a user experience so rich that it keeps people coming back time after time. If you own a smartphone and you're on social media, you know the feeling of picking up your phone and opening an app and not even knowing why. This is not an accident—this is by design. The people who design these apps use an artificial intelligence (AI)-based algorithm to test each change so that they can learn and adapt the app to get the best results. Social media companies are so agile, they're able to tweak and tinker with their platforms on the fly, around the clock.

Notifications are a great example of growth hacking. Your phone dings and you look at your phone. You open the notification, which takes you right to the comment or photo in which you are tagged. You don't have to work hard—it's frictionless. They make it so easy for you—so easy that you do it over and over again. Each time you answer a ding from your phone, you get a shot of dopamine. Dopamine is the reward neurotransmitter. It activates the pleasure center in the brain. Every time you repeat this same process, you are rewarded with good feelings. Before you know it, it soon becomes a habit.

Your likes and interests are also recorded and used to create curated content in your feed specific to your personal taste. The videos you see, the ads you are bombarded with, are all chosen by AI to get the desired message-to-market match. They know you better than you know yourself. Ensuring that your content is relevant and customized to you is one of the most powerful engagement strategies.

A third tactic these growth hackers use is the use of ellipses—those three blinking dots that indicate someone is typing a response to your direct message. Without ellipses, messaging would be more like email where you send out your message and look for a response the next time you check your phone. But… if you see that the person on the other end is responding that very minute, you are more likely to keep the app open and your phone out a little longer. It keeps you on the hook.

Even the people who design these features and work with the user experience are susceptible to its power. It's not like a magic trick that doesn't fool you once you know the secret. These features go right to the heart of how human beings are wired—they're pitting our own brains against us. Several of the former employees in the social media documentary admitted to having a phone addiction. They'd come home from work knowing exactly why they couldn't put their phone down, yet still had trouble kicking the habit. One individual went so far as to write himself a piece of software to help wean him from his social media dependence.

With our brains being hacked by the apps on our phones, we're left with only remnant bits of attention for our actual human interactions.

Phones are here to stay and will continue to be a source of distraction well into the future. For us to engage and capture the attention of the people we want to communicate and influence, we have to learn to be more engaging than our mobile phones.

When I'm not working for our clients at trade shows or training sales teams on engagement, I occasionally perform magic at events. It's good for me to get back to my first love and shake off the cobwebs.

Last winter during the holiday season, I donated my time at a free community dinner for people who might need some extra cheer at that time of the year. This dinner was a way to support people who might be having a hard time making ends meet. The event took place in a church basement—dozens of round tables set with red paper napkins. I roamed from table to table, entertaining guests after they were finished their meals.

If you've ever experienced table side close-up magic, you know it's something special. Seeing magic happen just inches from your nose, or sometimes right in your own hands, can be quite a thrill. As I made my way around the room, people were waving me down, asking me to come to their table next.

I approached one table of two parents and three children. The younger two kids were male and about 7 and 9 years old and the third was female and older—around 12 or 13. From the first moment when I interrupted their conversation to introduce myself, it was clear I'd have my hands full if I were to engage this older child in my magic. Her eyes were pasted to her phone screen and her fingers were furiously typing.

You would think that being open to watching magic is a no-brainer, but over the years I have learned that you need to "sell" the experience first. I put special emphasis on "sell" because, to be fair, many people have seen bad magic and it's not their idea of fun. Sometimes you must convince your audience to give you a chance—show your personality and hit them with a strong opening effect. Typically, after you've wowed them once, they are yours for the duration.

Upon getting the go ahead from 80% of the table, I noticed the teenager hadn't even looked up from her phone. Now, normally when someone approaches a group of people that you are part of and addresses the entire group, you at least look up to see who it is. Not this time. *No matter*, I thought, and pressed on.

I chose one of the younger siblings to help with a trick. The boy participated big time—playing along and laughing at all the right places. I glanced over to my right and the teenager still had her head down, ignoring the action at the table. By the time I'm three tricks in, I'm starting to get a little annoyed. In my head I'm thinking, *I'm doing miracles over here and you haven't even noticed!*

By now her parents were on her case too. "Chloe! Did you see that? Get off your phone and watch this guy."

Of course, this made her dig in even deeper, frowning at their interference.

I've been performing magic since I was five years old, so when I'm confronted with a challenge I like to rise to the occasion— even if it sometimes blows up in my face. I took a chance and asked Chloe to choose one of her hands for my next trick. Looking up, she reluctantly volunteered her right hand. I asked her to make a fist. I then proceeded to draw a small X on my own right hand with a Sharpie. Next, I gave her father a fist-bump; he fist-bumped his son, and it continued in this way to the mom, to the second son, and finally over to Chloe's waiting fist. She opened her hand, and there on her palm was the X in black Sharpie ink. Her jaw dropped and her demeanor completely changed. She was in a state of disbelief, shaking her head and trying to rub off the permanent marker ink. She'd finally been won over! I used a magic effect that took place right in this girl's own hand and—until after a good hand washing—that will be with her for some time.

To capture your audience's attention, I don't expect you to do magic. But there are other tricks and strategies you can use that are easy to learn and implement. Throughout this book, you'll be learning various engagement tactics you can use to start off on the right foot and ensure that your communication is landing and being understood. You will learn how to break through preoccupation and hack someone's attention just like those apps I talked about earlier—only in this case, we will be keeping people in the real world instead of taking them down a social media rabbit hole.

Going first

If you want to get someone excited, what do you need to do? Be excited first. If you want someone to relax, you need to be relaxed first. Our world is littered with examples of *entrainment*, where one subject can influence others merely with their presence. This effect is called Huygens's principle, based on the research of a Dutch scientist who placed a collection of pendulum clocks on the wall and noted that gradually all the pendulums synchronized their motions. Nature tends to synchronize itself, and like the clocks, we, too, can become synchronized with those around us. Even the father of Ericksonian hypnosis, Milton Erickson, stated that he would put himself into a trance first in order to induce a trance in others.

Therefore, if you want your audience to be captivated and present, you need to be captivated and present first. The more you can create a desired state in yourself, the more others will be positively affected around you.

During my magic performance for the family around the holiday dinner table, in order for them to be engaged and focused on me, I had to be engaged and highly focused on them first. By going first, I elicited the state that I wanted to create in myself so that I could create the same state in others. I went first and then they followed.

Try this the next time you run into a friend in the street. Make a conscious effort to be fully present in the moment, and then watch how this changes not only how they perceive you but what it demands of them. No distractions, no time constraints—it's just you and them, and that's all that exists.

In Olivia Fox Cabane's book, *The Charisma Myth*,[1] the author defines charisma as a combination of three characteristics: presence, power, and warmth. Just by being more present and holding that

---

[1] O. F. Cabane, *The Charisma Myth: How anyone can master the art and science of personal magnetism* (2011).

as an intention for yourself in your social interactions, you are cultivating charisma and making yourself more magnetic.

Of course, "going first" requires practice. It requires the desire to improve as well as mindfulness every time you enter a conversation or meeting. As homework for your next meeting, write down "Presence" on a sticky note and take it with you into your meeting. Or, if it is a virtual meeting, stick it to your monitor where it is easy to see and act as a reminder.

Test your material

One of the reasons that professional entertainers are so engaging is that they've mastered their craft. They have spent thousands of hours in the pursuit of excellence. They've studied, worked, and rehearsed to create a certain effect. In those hours of practice and performance, they've learned to alter their behavior to bring about the desired results. In entertainment, the feedback that the performer gets for their efforts makes their success (or failure) self-evident. There's applause, laughter, or perhaps—in a dramatic performance—tears. In this way, entertainers know that what they're doing is working, and they remember how to repeat this for each subsequent performance.

In his book *Outliers*, Malcom Gladwell coined "The-ten- thousand-hour rule."[2] This referred to the amount of time required to becoming a master in one's chosen field. Take chess, for example; by the time a person becomes a grand master at chess, they have spent a minimum of 10,000 hours studying the game.

Working as a trade show infotainer, I've performed at over 200 trade shows. My job is to stop people as they walk up and down the aisles and to build a massive crowd around my client's booth. I then communicate the client's value proposition and lead the interested attendees deeper into the booth, where their badges can be scanned and a demo can be given by one of the subject matter experts from the company.

---

[2] M. Gladwell, *Outliers: The story of success* (2008).

When I first started out, I quickly realized how hard it was to get people to just stop and watch what I was doing. It is difficult to build a crowd without getting those first few people to stop. I soon learned which approaches worked and which ones I should discard. If people stopped and stayed, I had done something right. If they left mid-performance, perhaps there was something I could have done differently. I became a product of my environment and quickly integrated the learning that resulted from each interaction. Feedback was my friend.

For you, it will be no different. You might discover a joke or greeting that is useful to capture people's attention at the start of a meeting. You might notice that people really like seeing you draw out your solution on the back of a napkin. There's a myriad of gambits, choices, and bits of business you can use to engage others immediately.

Your job now is to start being aware of what's working and what isn't. You may choose to write out a short AAR or After Action Report (a term borrowed from the military) following each business meeting or presentation. For every trade show I work at, I write out what I learned, what I liked, and what is still lingering. Reflecting on what worked well, what I'd do differently next time, and what remains unresolved and may need to be addressed in the future, helps me debrief the experience. These points are not only useful for future reference, but the act of writing down my findings helps me sort and sift my material. Self-assessments are key to understanding where I am at with your skills.

You may not be able to generalize one approach for the entire public; keep in mind how people like to be treated. In Tony Alessandro's book, *The Platinum Rule*, he explains that we shouldn't treat people the way we want to be treated (which is the Golden Rule), we should treat people the way *they* want to be treated; so, in your AARs, noting who responded to what can be valuable for future interactions.[3]

---

[3] T. Alessandra and M. J. O'Connor, *The Platinum Rule: Discover the four basic business personalities and how they can lead you to success* (1996).

When we engage with people who give us what we want, we are all eyes and all ears. We like those who give us what we want. So, each time you go into a social interaction, be aware of what you are doing, notice what works, and keep testing that hypothesis. Just like the social media platforms, we too can find what people like and adjust ourselves accordingly as we learn to evolve and become more engaging.

Chapter 3
A different AI

The first time I heard about artificial intelligence (AI), I was 14 years old, and I was watching the movie *Terminator 2: Judgment Day*. Released in the 1990s, the movie featured self-aware machines that lack empathy and take over the world. The field of AI in the real world, however, is more about machine learning, adapting, and making intelligent choices to enhance applications and reduce human input.

In her book *Alexa Is Stealing Your Job: The Impact of Artificial Intelligence on Your Future*, Rhonda Scharf predicts that by the year 2030, everything from data entry and bookkeeping to proofreading and retail sales will be replaced by AI.[1] While companies that use AI enjoy the benefits of cost savings and efficiencies, it also means fewer human-to-human interactions in our day-to-day lives. Even now, it's possible to go to the store or bank without making eye contact or speaking with anyone. With fewer chances to interact with others, not only are our social and communication skills bound to get soft, we feel less connected as we lose our sense of community. Humans weren't meant to exist in a bubble of

---

[1] R. Scharf, *Alexa Is Stealing Your Job: The impact of artificial intelligence on your future* (2019).

isolation, but unfortunately that's the trend we are seeing with advances in technology.

In Japan, there is a growing segment of the population known as *hikikomori*, which is defined as a recluse who withdraws from all social contact. Today there are over half a million modern-day hermits living in Japan, though experts believe the real number is much higher. The actual cause of this has not been determined, but many people blame addictions to video games and social media as the culprits. This lonely, lost generation of Japanese society may be the canary in the coal mine for other areas of the world as technology is more readily adopted across the world.

Whether it is self-induced isolation or just the easiest way to check out at the supermarket, society is faced with a growing problem that will ultimately result in a loss of interpersonal skills—and that's assuming you developed any in the first place. Several of my colleagues in business have shared with me that their teenage children are aware that they aren't very good at interacting with others. This is due to more than just the expected awkwardness that comes with adolescence. These teens simply have not had practice at interaction—they've been heads down, typing on their phones instead of being out with friends like their parents' generation.

In business there is also a problem brewing. Several of the sales leaders I've interviewed on my podcast have shared how they believe there is a Sales Apocalypse looming. This sales doomsday scenario is brought on by the younger generations of sales professionals.

Typically, the junior sellers are the ones on the phone talking to prospects and booking meetings for the more experienced business development managers (BDMs). In some companies these appointment-setting representatives have only been sending automated email campaigns. They don't get on the phone and talk about their company's solution. Not only are they *not* talking about the company, but they aren't getting real-time feedback on how they are doing with the prospect. They aren't getting rejected to their face (what not to do), but they also aren't getting any positive feedback on their engagement skills (what they're doing right). As these junior sellers "graduate" to the more senior BDM roles where face-to-face selling is required, we are going to see a whole generation of salespeople lacking interpersonal communication skills that we took for granted only a short while ago.

The entry level sales development representatives—who are tasked with phoning and emailing leads—are phoning less and just emailing. I see these reps in my client's booths and they have no experience talking about what their company does when face-to-face with a prospect.

Practice is how we learn. As a magician from the age of five, I recognized that learning sleights and appearing to do the impossible **is** possible with hard work and focus. I also recognized that when a person first tries something and fails, it is hard to get back on the horse, metaphorically speaking. The next time the opportunity presents itself, many of us may be reticent about taking another chance, but continual practice and refinement is necessary for honing skills.

Without these skills, without authentic interactions, what would the world be like? Our sense of empathy stems from the stimulation of our mirror neurons—brain cells that respond equally when we perform an action and when we witness someone else perform the same action. If we don't have opportunities to interact with others and use our mirror neurons, we could lose the ability to be empathetic. A world without human empathy would be a scary place indeed.

We need to find ways to use these soft skills, increase opportunities for face-to-face interactions, and enjoy the connection and camaraderie we feel when we engage with others.

Authentic interactions—the AI we need

Part of my role at our company has been to work as an infotainer at our various clients' trade show booths. Our presentations attract leads and much-wanted attention to our client's brand, booth, and people.

If you've never been to a big tech trade show, believe me, it's quite a sight. Some of the attractions I've seen include booths that incorporate structures like a skateboard half-pipe and a bicycle-powered Ferris wheel. Celebrity appearances are also a big deal. I once had "The Mountain" from *Game of Thrones* appearing several booths behind me, skateboarder Tony Hawk at the IBM booth beside me, and basketball player Klay Thompson of the Golden State Warriors in the corner of the same hall—all at the same time. Companies will go all out to grab the spotlight and create interest.

For me to fulfill my promise to a client, I must assemble a crowd of people in front of my client's booth. It all begins with one person. If I can convince one person to stop and engage with me, then I can start to build a crowd by involving others in the festivities.

One time in Chicago, I did just that. The presentation stands out in my mind because it was one of the most diverse crowds I've ever had—a unique mix of people from all over the world, representing different cultures and languages. Although there were many differences among them, they were sharing a common experience as a group. I had them focused on my magic and they were having a ball, high-fiving one another, smiling, laughing, and living in the moment.

Once a crowd has been won over and people drop their guard, they become a small community for as long as my presentation lasts. They laugh with each other, they move with each other and, in some cases, they breathe together—acting as a single entity.

When the show was over, people came over and thanked me. They went into the client's booth with an improved mental state, riding the high that the experience created. None of this would have been possible without someone taking a chance and engaging with another person. Taking sincere interest in someone and connecting in a meaningful way involves seeing that person as an individual and really hearing them. Being recognized as an individual fills us up, and obviously captures our attention. So, what we need more of in life and in business are **authentic interactions**.

To take advantage of the economies of scale, many businesses have used various tools to personalize and reach their target audience. When customer relationship management (CRM) software first came into use, businesses were able to mail-merge a person's name into a mass email. Organizations began to customize their communications to garner attention while reaching a large audience at the same time.

This approach has continued. At the time of this writing, there are several services that enable you to do mass outreach on LinkedIn. Every day, I get connection requests from "people" who tend to say the exact same thing in their connection requests—and when I check their profiles, invariably they are attempting to sell me something. I must admit, I'm guilty of this approach myself; however, what I've found is that the connections you create by using a personal touch—thoughtful requests written for a specific person and purpose—are always accepted and real conversations follow. Goodwill built by a one-to-one conversation has a much greater chance of resulting in business.

Being genuine or sincere isn't something that can be easily scaled to the masses. While there's a slew of new AI software that enable salespeople to be more effective, the bottom line is—you just can't fake sincerity. What is true for one person may not be true for another, and treating people as prospects and numbers is a big part of the problem. Even the word prospect carries a tone of insincerity. Words have power, so saying "potential client" instead of "prospect" creates an enormous shift in the energy contained within the words. "Prospect" feels like a faceless number, while "potential client" has the ring of value and care.

Many years ago, Dale Carnegie taught that if you want people to take an interest in you, you must first take an interest in them. Taking an interest in another person means finding out more about the person and being curious about what makes that person tick. These concepts are not new. Carnegie's book *How to Win Friends and Influence People* was published in 1936 and the concepts in it are still true today.[2]

We know so much more about brain science and how humans interact than we did in 1936 and we can apply that understanding to these age-old principles. Authentic interactions are borne out of genuine interest and the willingness to engage with one another. The connections brought about through this process create emotions which cement the events with a memorable stamp.

Three steps to creating connection through authentic interaction

Connect through commonalities

Sometimes stating something that is obvious to everyone is a great way of immediately connecting to another person or a group. Once I was on a very narrow escalator with a group of strangers in the Atlanta Convention Center. Each stair was only a little wider than my hip width. I commented to those around me that I was glad that the stairs weren't any narrower. The entire group let out a chuckle and chimed in with their own comments about the extreme narrowness of the escalator.

The more we are alike, the more we like the other person. Seeing a commonality—or in the example above, a common situation—links us to each other. When I am traveling internationally and see a fellow Canadian (perhaps identified by a maple leaf on a backpack), I have no problem striking up a conversation. Just knowing that we share a similar culture, value system, and prime minister instantly bonds us. This type of connection occurs often in a foreign location because the fact that we are both fish-out-of-the-water strongly draws us to each other.

---

[2] D. Carnegie, *How to Win Friends and Influence People* (1936).

Commonalities can range from birthplace and common friends to body language and vocal tone. Any commonality can work to move us into an authentic interaction.

One summer, I was at a city park with my family when I happened to see a man dressed exactly like me. From our T-shirts advertising an obscure beverage to the khaki shorts, the coincidence was amazing. At first, I snuck up behind him and my wife covertly took a picture. Then I decided I would approach him and point out our twin looks. When he saw me, the connection was instant and we shared a good laugh. Two strangers sharing personal space as if they are lifelong friends. This can happen in an instant with strong commonalities.

Connection before conversion

The term *business relationship* is backwards. The relationship must come before the business. In some scenarios, there are unspoken rules about when you can get down to business. When golfing in a corporate setting, for example, it is inappropriate to talk business until the back nine—meaning, you must wait until halfway through your round of golf before even broaching the subject.

Once rapport is firmly in place, work on deepening the connection by learning more about the person you're with. Some might find it a cliché, but the saying is applicable and bears repeating: "People don't care what you know, until they know you care." One of my favorite questions to cut right to the heart of what people are about is: "I'm curious, what passion projects have you been working on lately?"

This is a great question that helps you get to know what someone is all about. Depending on the person, the question may be interpreted in any number of ways—a hobby or sport, a non-profit organization they lead or participate in, or a book in the making.

Unless you have a mind like a steel trap, you would be well-advised to write down the things you learn in a notebook or a CRM system after the interaction. Some people feel that keeping notes in this way is cheating or manipulative, but it is not. In fact, caring enough about what you learn to put pen to paper says something about you. When you reconnect with that person and ask questions about those same topics, they will be appreciative of your thoughtfulness.

Act as if

I have been hired as an entertainer at countless events where I dined with the attendees, requiring me to make conversation with complete strangers. One of the tricks I learned for creating conversation and getting to know people quickly was to ask about their work or hobbies, and then *act as if* I was the most interested person in the world. Sometimes this was easy (talking with a SWAT team door breacher) and sometimes it was not (chatting with an accountant). What I discovered was that if I acted *as if* I was interested and asked a few questions, very soon I would be genuinely fascinated—much to my counterpart's delight.

What is even easier is to ask someone how they became interested in their particular subject matter. That question was frequently a shortcut to connection. The reason behind any given choice is often more relatable than the choice itself. It's not surprising that the answers I get to this question often had analogous examples in my own life experience, resulting in instant rapport.

Chapter 4
Dare to engage

E ngagement: *to occupy, attract or involve someone's interest or attention.*

Before we can communicate, sell, persuade, or woo, we must have the willingness to engage. To engage another person, one must initiate, make the first move. This willingness to engage is risky, of course. We have to put ourselves out there, take a chance and risk looking foolish.

Willingness to engage is not innate; as humans, we are naturally risk averse. We are wired to play it safe and avoid stress. Our brains are designed to protect us and to ensure the survival of the species. All animals naturally understand this. Among most primates, direct eye contact is an implied threat and is used to assert dominance and display aggression.

This way of survival also works in the concrete jungle. In Lindsay Buckley's *How to Survive the New York City Subway*, she writes, "Do not, under most any circumstances, lock eyes with someone else on the train.[1] If you accidentally make eye contact with a 'normal'

[1] L. Buckley, *How to Survive the New York City Subway* (2014). Available from https://matadornetwork.com/nights/nyc-subway-survival-guide/ [accessed May 23, 2025].

New Yorker, they will instantly shift their gaze away. But if it's a 'crazy' New Yorker, eye contact is like an invitation to their crazy." To avoid getting caught up in someone else's drama, New Yorkers have adapted by avoiding interactions.

But in the business world, this focus on survival works against us. Our survival instinct tells us to stay in our own bubbles and keep to ourselves, but the downside of that instinct is that it also separates us from others. The larger the community, the more our survival instinct kicks in, as our brain tells us we are surrounded by potential threats to our existence.

I found this out firsthand, growing up in a town of just 500 people. Everybody knew everybody. It was a great place to grow up. I could go for a bike ride around the entire town and be back in 15 minutes. The business section was up on a hill, so "downtown" was really "uptown." No traffic lights—just stop signs and one fancy intersection with a four-way stop.

When you grow up in a community where people don't even lock their doors at night, you tend to give strangers the benefit of the doubt. We would say "hi" and wave to everybody and anybody. If a strange car drove by while you were out walking your dog, you'd wave—you might not recognize the car or the person inside, but you'd wave anyway, just in case one of your neighbors had bought a new car and you didn't recognize them. You didn't want to appear stuck up. It was an insurance wave, and it made visitors to our small village feel welcome and at home.

One of our town residents, Glen Couling, fully embraced this welcoming everybody and everyone philosophy. Everyone in town called him Smokey, and he owned the gas station on main street. He owned and rode horses, was bow-legged, had bad knees, and walked with a certain swagger; he was the closest thing our town had to a cowboy. But what really set Smokey apart was his colorful way of greeting the people he knew.

I delivered papers with my best friend, Sean, and if we saw Smokey uptown, he'd give us a big, wide, arching wave that could barely be contained by his small half-ton truck cab. He was known around the town for his gigantic wave. Smokey was a friendly guy who was authentic and loved to make his presence known and people feel welcomed.

That was the world I grew up in. No reason to mistrust anyone, and plenty of reasons to interact and see what was happening around town.

After graduating from high school, I moved to a university residence in the "big city" of Brandon, Manitoba. At the time, Brandon had a population of 50,000—100 times bigger than where I'd come from.

Living in a dorm was a lot like living in a small town. You would see the same people every day and find yourself in circumstances where you could talk with them—in class, in the cafeteria, in the common room during the evenings. If you wanted to know what was happening that night and where the best party was, you asked around, you inquired. You engaged.

After graduating, I moved to Winnipeg, a city with over half a million people. I found an apartment building close to downtown that had a similar look to my university dorm. I felt very at home— that is, until I met my neighbors.

Each time I passed a neighbor in the hall, I would stop to chat and would often be rewarded with some polite conversation. But there was always awkwardness to these interactions. Eventually, these conversations downgraded to just an exchange of "hi" in the hallway or elevator. Then one day, there seemed to be a decision of sorts on the part of my various neighbors to dispense with all the pleasantries. I'm not sure if the honeymoon period of being new to the building was over for me, or if I just began to wait for the other person to make the first move. It felt as if we had never met before. Like they didn't remember me from months ago. And it wasn't just in my apartment building that I experienced the cold shoulder. When greeting people in the street or simply making eye contact and smiling, I soon discovered that few people would reciprocate my greeting.

Eventually, I became a city dweller. I kept to myself, did my own thing, and kept my eyes down. I had stopped trying to engage because I had become preoccupied with things inside my own bubble, but I also felt beat down by the lack of response I got from other people.

When I moved into a house, I decided I was going to change how I communicated. They say you choose the house you buy, but you don't get to choose your neighbors. Still, being willing to interact is the neighborly thing to do. Saying "hi" when you see them over the fence, waving to them, or helping them out where you can. It's these interactions that allow us to get to know people and form real bonds—whether those bonds end up leading to true friendship, or just occasionally borrowing tools or a cup of sugar.

One day on a business trip, pondering this idea of initiating interactions and daring to engage, I decided to play a little game. While walking through the airport, how many people could I make eye contact with? I would give people a smile and see who would respond. By now, I had been fully conditioned by city life and so my expectations were low—but the odd person did return my gaze and smile. We didn't stop or even speak, but we connected. People may have thought I was a weirdo or that I was being too forward, but whatever meaning they may have attached to my actions is irrelevant. In that moment of their smile triggered by mine, they felt acknowledged—just like my wave from my bike, or Smokey's arching welcome made strangers in my small town feel like they were seen.

Everyone just wants to be seen and heard. Being acknowledged means we matter—that we exist. Through engagement, we have the ability to impact another person's thoughts, feelings, and actions. We can positively impact the trajectory of someone's day, and while the angle of that trajectory may be fleeting, for a certain person in a certain place in life, the effect may be profound.

On the same day at the same airport, I stopped to eat at a sports bar. The sign read *Seat Yourself*, so I glanced around the restaurant looking for an ideal spot. Still thinking about engagement,

I deliberately chose a long high-top table. The table had seating for six, which meant that a stranger could, potentially, sit directly across from me. In only a matter of minutes, that's exactly what happened.

Emboldened by the "social research" that I was covertly conducting, I decided to strike up a conversation with this new dining partner. At first glance, I could see he was married and in his mid-forties. He wore a baseball hat with camouflage on it, which clued me that he might be the outdoorsman type. I asked him where he was headed, and he responded, "Louisville."

We chatted casually for the duration of our meals. I find that people traveling alone are often quite open to conversation. They are in the same boat as you and are looking for a way to pass the time between flights.

It turns out we were both reading books about mental resilience authored by former Navy Seals, we were both business owners facing the challenges of scaling our businesses, and we even ended up both ordering the fish tacos. The similarities we discovered during our interaction further bonded us. Now, don't get me wrong—we were different in plenty of ways, but because I set myself up to engage and initiated the first question, we were able to pass the time, enjoy some companionship and learn more about one another.

This chapter is titled "Dare to engage" because we must challenge ourselves to do more and to go against some of our natural instincts—in some cases, our learned protective behaviors. But on the other side of that challenge, you'll find connection and the joy of sharing in the human experience. That might sound like a lofty statement, but if you have ever traveled and experienced different places and cultures, you know the joy and sense of commonality that is possible with people you have just met.

Whether you are reading this book because you are in sales and marketing, interested in human dynamics, or just shy and looking for a way to connect, there's a reward on the other side of engagement. And the more you engage, the more you will want to engage. The reward is so nourishing and fulfilling that it is worth it to train yourself to be more of who you are, and to share that with the world.

So instead of doing what's easy or doing what you've always done, push yourself—get out of your social comfort zone and dare to engage!

Dare to engage challenges

To exercise our engagement muscles, it's necessary to go out there and get some reps in. Here are three ideas to increase your daring.

Play the smile game

Next time you're at the mall, in an airport, or just going for a stroll, see how many people you can get a smile from. It's an interesting experiment in making eye contact and non-verbal communication.

When my daughter was a baby, my wife and I would take walks with our overloaded stroller chock full of baby supplies and toys. We would get all kinds of smiles from other parents who knew exactly what we were going through. Now that my kids are older, I find myself doing the same thing to other first-time parents, giving them a knowing smile when I see them pushing their little ones around knowing exactly what they are going through.

To convey the right intention here and not come across as creepy, a helpful tip: When making eye contact and attempting to connect with someone, try to really see that person and all the good that is in them. Try to see them for who they are without judgment. I find that with these intentions in mind, my smile comes from a place of greater authenticity—not fake or creepy. It's a smile that expresses love for fellow humans.

(Note: Trust your instincts here. Not everyone feels safe smiling at strangers. Pick a time and a place where it is low risk to experiment with upping your warmth and approachability. A trade show is a perfect place to test this out.)

Nod of Respect

Is the smiling thing too much for you? Try the tamed-down, tip-of-the-hat version, which I like to call the Nod of Respect. This is useful for situations where the smile is too much or too risky.

First off, I want to emphasize how small this gesture can be. With only eye contact and a tiny nod, you can acknowledge another person and show respect to someone you may not typically greet or interact with.

As a man, I often use this as a micro-greeting to other men. The tougher they appear, the more they seem to appreciate it.

On my walk to work, there are often people working the line of cars at some of the intersections along the way looking to receive some spare change. I recognize that they're fighting for their survival and many of them had a hard life. Instead of ignoring them like people are often inclined to do, I'll use the Nod of Respect—and I usually get one back.

Cashier compliment

Instead of opting for the self-checkout, go old school and interact with a cashier. They see many people in a day and not all of them are pleasant. Challenge yourself to not only make them smile but make their day. A sincere compliment can have a person walking home on a cloud.

If not a compliment, see how your interaction can interrupt the pattern they see all day long. Any out of the norm, fun, or playful jest is a welcomed change.

PART 2
ENGAGEMENT
BASICS

Chapter 5
Being an authority

Authority carries weight. When someone with credibility speaks, people pay attention. That's because the messenger can shape how the message is received. Authority isn't just about job titles or credentials—it's about presence, clarity, and the confidence to own your message. When done right, authority makes your words harder to dismiss and your message more likely to land.

Early in my career, I was a voracious reader of marketing strategies and tactics for entrepreneurs. Almost everything I read at the time was marketing related. Among the advice I discovered was that not only are testimonials and other forms of social proof important components of any sales letter or marketing piece, but that the person who is quoted is just as—or more—important than the quote itself. The more well-known a person is, the more impressive the testimonial. So, you could get a mediocre quote about your product or service from Kevin O'Leary of *Shark Tank*, and it would be valuable simply because your business has been mentioned by a Shark.

However, there's a caveat. Being a known commodity doesn't mean your opinion carries weight on all subjects. For example, a social media influencer who is known for fashion advice may not influence me when it comes to the best way to play golf or the most fuel-efficient new car to purchase.

The 5 Ws of Authority

The 5 Ws of Authority can be summarized in almost the same way a journalist tells a news story. The 5 Ws of Authority are only slightly different. "How" replaces "When" because authority is established in the present moment—people want to know how you are an authority and why they should listen *right now*. "How" brings immediacy, action, and clarity to your message, making it more engaging and relevant.

Who?

The "who" is your name, your title, what you are known for. If you're a CEO of a company, that gives you credibility; if you're the CEO of a well-known brand, even more so. Professional designations—with letters such as CPA, PhD, PEng, following your name—also create instant credibility. Even if someone has never heard of you but knows you're a CEO or former military, you'll be that much further ahead in winning them over. Did you write a book, found a company, or run an ultra-marathon? All of these details go a long way to giving your audience a reason to listen.

What?

What have you done? What are your accomplishments? Have you climbed Mount Everest? Have you worn a nametag for 20 consecutive years, like Scott Ginsberg who you'll meet later in the book? The "what" is going to vary drastically from person to person. Highlighting your most relevant "what" for your audience is going to build your authority.

"What" also includes what people say about you. Influential words from others in positions of authority can dramatically elevate your own status. This social proof can be a powerful tool!

Where?

Authority can be subjective and dependent on context. Where an interaction takes place can alter the status dynamics and the authority you wield. A surgeon and a golf pro will have different perceived status depending on where they are. In a hospital, there's no doubt that the surgeon has the authority. On a golf course, the tables are turned and a golf pro's words will carry more weight and be listened to more carefully by anyone in their foursome.

I once unwittingly dressed down a CEO in front of his own employees. My company was hired to increase lead generation for a company exhibiting at the National Retail Federation show in New York. We were also tasked with training their booth staff to ensure they would be effective for the coming three days. In the first five minutes of the training, I noticed a man talking to his neighbors and frequently looking down at his phone. Just as any teacher would have, I called him out and asked him to pay careful attention to the presentation. The man apologized and asked me to continue. After the presentation I was informed that the man I'd admonished was the CEO.

Anyone who knows me knows that I'm not one for confrontation. Had I known who he was, I would never have dared to speak to him as I did. But the situation being what it was, I was in my element, communicating my expertise like I know how. I was solely focused on what I was hired to do.

Even though there was a tense moment when the rest of the employees in the room were holding their breath, waiting to see what would transpire, I earned the respect of the CEO, I was the authority in the room.

Why?

Why should I listen to you? This is what people might ask themselves. The "why" is the relevance you bring to the audience— the "What's In It For Me?" component of your message. Your authority hinges on being relevant in your communication because if what you say doesn't matter, why listen? Reminding your audience of what's at stake builds tension and reinforces why one needs to pay attention. Being on-point with benefit-oriented language that is tailored to your audience is how you increase your why-factor and create more authority.

How?

This is the way that you carry yourself—how you are as a person, a communicator, a speaker. Do you project your authority with confidence or do you tend to undermine your expertise and sell yourself short? Do you fully embrace who you are?

For most of us, this is the place where we can best increase our authority quotient. We can't change where we're from, who we are, and what we've done, but we can change how we go about representing ourselves in the moment. As both verbal and non-verbal communication say so much about who we are, it's in our best interest to be cognizant not just of the message but how we communicate that message to best convey the meaning.

How you are perceived by your audience will influence your ability to influence. What do you wear to convey the authority that you have? For some, it's a business suit, for others (often tech CEOs) it's a hoodie and sneakers.

Let's look at an example to see how these 5 Ws all work together.

I was recently booked to be the virtual emcee (MC) of a sales kick-off for a billion-dollar company. They had hired our company to create excitement and entertainment—and to provide contrast in an effort to re-engage attention spans in this virtual event.

One of my duties as the emcee was to introduce the keynote speaker, Francois Pienaar. I am well plugged into the professional speaking scene in North America and I had never heard of Francois Pienaar, I was initially unimpressed. However, I assumed he must be of a decent caliber if a billion-dollar company had hired him.

I needed to write an introduction for the speaker. As soon as I started doing research on Pienaar, I quickly realized that I really should have known who he was.

Francois Pienaar (who) is the former captain of the South African rugby team. As this fact suggests, he's from South Africa (where). In 1995, he led his team to a world championship (what). The mid-nineties in South Africa were tumultuous years—apartheid had just ended and Nelson Mandela was elected president.

The more I learned, the more I realized how influential this man had been. His team's world championship win had created a sense of pride in the country that was so very needed at that time. Then I learned that Matt Damon had played Francois Pienaar in the blockbuster movie *Invictus*, which also starred Morgan Freeman as Nelson Mandela.

I went from not thinking much of this guy to discovering that a movie had been made about how his team and Nelson Mandela had united the country through sport. His connection to Nelson Mandela gave Francois an immense amount of credibility. After what I had learned, I couldn't wait to hear what he had to say. His "why"—his relevant message—would relate to salespeople because of the competitive spirit needed to succeed in the business world. His message of unity and cooperation would play into any company's culture of diversity and inclusion.

So even before he had opened his mouth to speak, I was already intrigued. Then I learned that Mandela had said this about Pienaar: "Under his inspiring leadership a nation was brought together." With that powerful testimonial ("what" others say about you) you just know that this man had a story to tell.

In his presentation he came across (how) as genuine and humble. Dressed in a suit, he looked classy and professional. He exuded an air of gratitude for having played a part in South Africa's history.

Of course, we all don't have a back story like Mr. Pienaar, but perhaps we can learn from his example and cultivate authority for ourselves.

Why authority matters

Using the example above, if I had been a virtual attendee (and not the emcee), I might have had to make a choice about how to spend my time and energy. Whether it might have been taking a lunch break, or catching up on work emails, if the case hadn't been made about why Mr. Pienaar would be compelling to watch, I may have missed out on his inspiring story.

We are taught to listen to people with higher status than ourselves. We listen to our teachers, preachers, and politicians. We look to doctors when our health is at risk, and we seek the help of financial advisers when we are looking to invest.

But any one of those authority figures would be out of whack if certain criteria were not met.

Would you invest with a financial planner who isn't certified (who)? Would you listen to a doctor who's dressed in grubby clothes and doesn't wash their hands (how)? Would you trust a politician to represent your community if they had just moved there to try and win that seat (where)?

I think you get the idea. If any one of the 5 Ws is not fully satisfied, something will seem off.

Generating more authority

Let's look at how you can elevate your expertise and compel people to engage.

Maximizing your who

Write a bio for yourself. You know—the kind you might see on the inside of a book cover or hear an emcee say as an introduction. Think about how you would like to be introduced to an audience of people who've never heard of you. What have you accomplished, what's your educational background, where did you grow up, and so on.

Next, run it through a relevance filter. What do people really care about or what do they really need to know in order to understand who you are and the value that you bring? I frequently write introductions for speakers and industry experts, and I'm often amazed at how badly written their bios are. There's usually a whole lot of "so-what-who-cares" that needs to be deleted.

Don't get too wordy or self-aggrandizing—just say it in plain language and make it benefit-oriented. Write and rewrite that bio until it is hard-hitting and to-the-point. This is what people need to know about you. If they know this, they'll pay attention to the first words out of your mouth.

Use this bio to spice up your elevator pitch, your LinkedIn profile, and any place where it can help build a frame around who you are.

Maximizing your what

If you're serious about your career, I'm sure you value education and experience. Consistently reinvesting your time and money into education is a great way to increase your expertise. It's not just about what you've learned but also what you know. Consider writing a book to "celebra-tize" yourself and become a greater authority figure in your area of interest. In addition to books, publish articles and make yourself available for interviews, podcasts, and the like. Before you know it, you'll elevate your status in your industry.

What others say about you

The "what" component also refers to what people say about you. Aligning yourself with other celebrities can dramatically up the perception of your own status.

If you've been to Vegas, you know from the billboards that it is home to many professional magicians. One of them—Murray Sawchuk—is known as the Celebrity Magician. Before his show begins, a slide show is projected onstage. Slide after slide, you see photos of Murray with various celebrities, from Jerry Lewis and Larry King to Robin Leach and Jason Priestley. He's had his picture taken with literally hundreds of celebrities. Of course, he then shares quotes from these celebrities, praising him and his show. "Absolutely amazing—you're the best!" Murray's association to these celebrities elevates his own stock and enables him to differentiate himself from other magicians on the Las Vegas strip.

What have others said about you? Are they prominent figures? Check your LinkedIn endorsements and look for "pull quotes" by extracting the very best parts of the testimonials.

Don't have any testimonials? Get some. Reach out to one of your best customers and ask for a quote. Heck, some of them will even let you write it yourself—it saves them time and you get exactly what you want. Send an email politely asking for a testimonial and include one that you've pre-written as an example. If it sounds good and isn't too over the top, many people will just give you the go-ahead to use what you've written.

Use these testimonials in your bio, on your business card, your website, social media, your LinkedIn profile… you get the idea. Growing your authority really is about marketing and personal branding.

Social proof is the persuasion principle that Dr. Robert Cialdini coined in his ground-breaking book entitled *Influence: The Psychology of Persuasion*.[1] In the book, the author proves how people look to others for what they should do and think. The use of testimonials is a classic example of social proof.

Celebrities create social proof with their entourages. A group of people following a "leader" edifies that leader which, in turn, attracts more attention from others.

I'm no celebrity, but on the trade show floor I see social proof in action all the time. When you talk with one other person (two people), it's just a conversation. Add one more (three's company), and one more after that (four is a crowd). When you have a group of four people, it's a big enough gathering to be noticed. People

---

[1] Robert B. Cialdini, *Influence: The psychology of persuasion* (2007).

wonder what that small crowd is watching. The social proof created by others watching and enjoying something is enough to pique the interest of others walking by. As a crowd grows, it adds additional members more quickly. The bigger the crowd, the more powerful the pull. The more people listen to you, the more credibility you build.

This is why speaking opportunities are an effective way to build your authority.

Maximizing your why

As mentioned in the prior chapter, your relevance is what compels your audience to pay attention. Continue to frame your ideas around the things that your audience wants and needs, and also how they can avoid the things they don't want. Any time you feel your audience is starting to zone out, circle back on why you are there and why they should listen.

Maximizing your how

The way you carry yourself speaks volumes about who you are. In less than a fraction of a second, people will sum you up and put you in one of their categories. Once that first impression has been made, it's an uphill battle to convince others you are someone different than who they have already judged you to be. It's easier and more efficient to look the part and be congruous with their categorization.

When I travel to shows, I wear a suit. I do this for various reasons. For one, if my bag gets lost, I can use the Tide packet in my carry-on bag to wash the clothes I wore and be ready to work the following day. But there are other advantages besides being prepared for emergencies. If you get a first-class upgrade, you never know who you'll be seated next to. It might be a C-suite executive, a founder, a journalist, or another type of person who has the potential to further your goals.

Looking like a million bucks can get you closer to earning a million bucks

As I've mentioned, I prefer to work in a suit. I've tried more casual looks over the years, but it has never been quite as effective. I've found that if a speaker dresses better than their audience, the speaker can create a dynamic in which the audience members will defer to the speaker. This means that I can command a crowd much easier when I'm well dressed. In fact, people sometimes approach me in the booth, assuming I'm one of the company executives because I'm wearing a suit. While I hate to disappoint them, it does feel nice to be confused for a C-level executive of a billion-dollar company.

It's not just about what you wear but how you feel and move in those clothes. Looking good is often associated with feeling good. As my old hockey coach used to say about the team dress code, "If you look good, you'll feel good, and then you'll play good." My attire is directly linked to the state I want to have, or the "mode" that I'm in. When I put on my suit, I tend to move more purposefully. The suit is a physical reminder that I'm there to command attention.

Some might feel out of place in something too formal, but whatever the case is for you, I do recommend looking the part. While it seems to be in vogue to have young tech CEOs sporting jeans, a T-shirt, and a hoodie, I personally feel it hampers their authority. This clothing makes them look like everyone else and therefore many people will treat them like everyone else. Remember: standing out and employing contrast is important for capturing attention.

The way in which you speak is also very important to your authority. Do you project the confidence of an authority expert, or are you just putting things out there and just floating ideas? Your tone of voice can have a huge impact on your perceived competence.

Maximizing your where

The context in which you have authority will be limited. Just because you are well respected in one industry or vertical doesn't mean you'll have the same pull in another. If you're making an industry change or getting a job with a new company, you may need to tweak your bio and adjust how you frame your expertise.

Engagify is a great example. In our company, we went from working primarily with technology companies at trade shows—doing custom infotainment presentations for lead generation—to adding a new offering of teaching sales and marketing teams to be more engaging. We used our experience in creating engaging presentations in one of the most demanding environments (trade shows) as a testament to our skills. So while the offering is quite different, there's overlap and the prior experience supports the new context.

Identify any areas of overlap between your new position (or the field you wish to enter) and your prior experience. It does help to move to an adjacent field, or a slightly different vertical in the same industry, rather than make a full 180-degree change. For example, if you sell IT services in the cloud computing vertical, selling security software isn't too much of a departure.

In summary

While reading this chapter, did anything come up for you on how your authority may be perceived? Can you think of ways you could improve in this area to enhance your engagement? You may need to take inventory of your own 5 Ws. Look for areas that could be strengthened and consider the ways in which you can up your authority quotient.

Chapter 6
Relevance: the great equalizer

Have you ever had someone say to you "Can I pick your brain?" I get that often and I assume you get your share as well. It's a compliment of sorts because someone recognizes your expertise in a particular area, and they want to engage with you in order to gain some of your knowledge. (If *you* ever want to approach someone and ask this, I recommend the phrase "absorb your genius"—you'll have your request granted much more readily.) Thank you to my speaker colleague Stephanie Staples for this great reframe.

They've approached you because you're seen as an expert who has relevant information that will benefit them. Stacking authority and relevance together is a potent combination that creates nearly irresistible engagement.

Being relevant or "on-point" seems like a no-brainer, but it's often overlooked. What you think is important about a given topic is not necessarily what's important to the person you are engaging with. Relevance means being on the same page as your audience and always providing value.

If your message is irrelevant—you are just wasting time. If you're in sales and trying to get the attention of your prospect, your attempts at outreach will be completely ignored if you're not laser-focused on solving their actual problems. They'll never get on the phone with you if they don't believe you have a compelling offer that personally or professionally benefits them.

Often, we are guilty of making our communications about us instead of about them. We've all met a self-absorbed person who likes to go on about themselves and their accomplishments. In their minds, they're discussing the most fascinating topic in the world—themselves. However, for you, the conversation has quickly become boring. You tune out, thinking about unrelated topics and tasks you need to accomplish. That "tuning out" is precisely what we want to avoid in our own interactions. To keep our audiences interested, we must be relevant.

Relevancy is powerful. One of the ways my company has become the go-to solution for creating engaging trade show presentations is that we always make the client and the solution they offer the star of the show. Meanwhile, some trade show performers wonder why doing amazing tricks is not sufficient to get them booked. Entertainment is fun to watch but combining entertainment with the products and solutions that attendees have interest in brings it to the next level and makes it all about them.

One of the decisions I made early on in my trade show career was not to perform for applause. One of the primary reasons for this was that applause signifies an ending (closing of a story loop), and audience members will feel it's a good time to move on. If there is no applause, the audience remains in the moment for longer.

Applause is also a cue for a performer—especially a magician—to take credit for the "miracle" they've just presented. Applause makes it about the performer, not the audience. If someone does start to clap, however, I thank them but then explain that it's not necessary as "their attention is my applause."

As you can imagine, when you're paid to generate crowds of interested prospects, every detail of your presentation has to be carefully structured and choreographed to produce rapt attention. In fact, there are so many things going on in my presentations, I can't consciously manage them all at once. I've had to add each layer slowly over time so that eventually I manage many of the tasks and intentions of my performance unconsciously.

For example, a magic performance involves the audience in front of you (just one dull moment away from leaving), a script you've memorized in order to weave in the marketing message, the manipulation of the prop or trick that you're performing, projecting your voice so you can be heard over the din, remembering to breathe properly so as to not lose your voice by day three, and on top of all that, new elements to integrate into your performance on the fly—such as dealing with difficult audience members—all to keep the audience's eyes glued on the proceedings.

The choice of material is also critical. I perform several effects that have a built-in element of risk. The risk involves me either getting hurt or losing money. Both compel onlookers to watch and see what will happen.

For example, I remember one instance at the National Association of Broadcasters show in Las Vegas. NAB, as it's known, attracts 91,000 people and takes over the entire Las Vegas Convention Center (which is one of the largest convention centers in the world, with just under two million square feet).

I was in the middle of a presentation with a good-sized crowd and about to start my next segment when I looked up and saw a massive crowd at a booth a couple of aisles over. I always tell myself not to get "crowd envy," but the fact is a large crowd around a booth is a measurement of success and creates great optics for the exhibiting company.

I went on with my set, launching into one of my signature routines that never fails to bring in a big crowd: Russian roulette with staple guns. For this bit, I use four staple guns and load just one of them. I mix them up in a bag and then distribute them to four different spectators to hold. I then rely on their collective intuition to select the safe staple guns, while I speak about the risks that can be avoided by making the safe choice to work with my client. At the end of the routine I have two staple guns to my temples and a couple of apprehensive volunteers worried for my safety. I'm telling you, it's pretty hard to walk by without stopping to watch.

As usual, the routine doubled my crowd, but it still paled in comparison to the one I could see from my stage, two aisles over. *What are they doing over there?* I thought to myself, *I'm risking life and limb over here, going all out, doing everything I can to make the show exciting and compelling. I've got to see for myself what they are doing.*

After my set, I walked over to the booth in question to try and discover the source of my crowd envy. Much to my dismay, there was no entertainment, no high-stakes raffle for a car, not even attractive booth models—just a regular guy doing a demo of the company's technology. He wasn't outgoing or engaging—in fact, he was committing a number of presenter faux pas—but none of that seemed to matter to his audience.

Once the presentation ended and the crowd dissipated, I went up to the booth and asked a staff member why they were attracting such a large crowd. "That's just our normal demo that we're showing off," he said, "Our technology is new and gaining a lot of momentum, so it's generating a lot of interest."

How humbling it was to discover that a lifetime of performance expertise couldn't compete with an uninspired demonstration of new technology from an up-and-coming company. It was in that instant that I realized: relevance reigns supreme. The right message for the right audience at the right time cannot be beat.

Relevance is the great equalizer. It's like feeding a starving crowd of people. The food doesn't have to be from a four-star Michelin restaurant, it just has to satiate hunger—and in that sense, almost any food will do.

So why is relevance so powerful?

As it turns out, it's the way we're wired. As a matter of survival, we are tuned into whatever can be of benefit to us. Evolutionarily, a benefit would be something like finding a mate or food, or it could mean avoiding any danger that could potentially bring us harm. Our brain is wired to protect us so that we can go on living and propagate the species.

After hundreds of thousands of years of evolution, the rewards and dangers have changed, but the wiring remains. For our brains to bring us to conscious attention, they must see the potential of a given reward/novelty (the neurotransmitter dopamine) or be aware of a threat/stress (the neurotransmitter norepinephrine). These two neurochemicals are the keys to capturing attention.

At *Engagify*, when we train sales teams on engagement skills, we tell them it's all about keeping your content "U-Focused." In other words, the content must be about the audience if the audience is to care about the message you're communicating. Everyone is always tuned into their favorite radio station: WIIFM (What's In It For Me?).

When you run your content through this filter, it helps you decide what's truly important. Ask yourself: Is this a problem or threat that my audience may experience now or in the future? What are some of the solutions they could use to avoid this fate?

In order to have relevance, your information must contain a pay-off for the recipient. Back in 2016, I was walking the trade show floor at VM World in San Francisco when I saw four individuals in a booth, dressed in green screen suits (except in this case they were blue suits). Suddenly, dance music started blaring from the booth's loud speakers, and these four blue-spandex-clad mascots started dancing like robots. It was quite a scene. Everyone in the vicinity stopped what they were doing and took notice. However, the moment the song ended, everything returned to normal. People walked away and went back to whatever they were previously doing. It was like one long, awkward moment. No one went into the booth, no leads were acquired by the exhibiting company, and no one learned about the company's solution. The stunt was a meaningless distraction with zero relevance.

Capturing attention without the proper intention comes off as desperate and deceitful

So how do we become relevant? How can we ensure that we aren't just sound and fury like the example above?

To be relevant, you must show that you understand your audience. If you can pace their experience and their pains, they will give you the time of day and the benefit of the doubt. It's like the old adage "Nobody cares what you know until they know how much you care." If you ask people how they are doing, they can't help but answer. You are immediately relevant because of the interest you've taken in them. Your outreach is you-focused.

If you're in a business setting, ask intelligent, probing questions about the challenges the company might be facing, instead of the staid, stale and stock questions sales people tend to ask, like "What keeps you up at night?"

When I'm working at a trade show, I'll give the people watching my presentation a scenario in which I describe someone who's similar to them, experiencing similar frustrations due to similar problems. While raising my hand, I'll ask, "How many people here have ever felt this way?" Hands go up and heads nod and immediately I know that my presentation is going to connect with this audience because the remaining content solves the problem I've raised. First, my presentation will be pushing the stress neurotransmitter button as we wallow in the problem, then it will cause a dopamine spike as we reveal a new and better way of solving the problem.

As each piece of content is delivered, I'm looking for feedback to ensure that it's hitting home. The same strategy is applicable to everyday business conversations. Pay attention to the feedback. Is someone sending body language that indicates they may be zoning out? Were you talking about yourself or your company just now? If so, refocus focus and make it about them once again.

Ask questions!

One of the easiest ways to shift focus back to your audience or counterpart is to ask a question. This makes a person feel good because they get to speak, but at the same time it gives the questioner control of the direction and pace of the conversation. Want to speed up the interaction? Ask close-ended questions (yes/no). Want to dig deeper and learn more? Ask open-ended questions (what/why/how).

Here's a quick relevance test for emails or presentation transcripts: Count the number of times the words "you" and "yours" appear and compare them to the appearances of "me", "my", and "our." Chances are, you're talking about yourself more than about your recipient. Rewrite the email or sales copy to better reflect your audience. Not only will it get their attention more effectively, it will allow them to see themselves in your written copy and immerse them more fully into your stories.

One of the best ways to be more relevant is to ask for feedback from someone whose opinion you trust. The older I get, the one thing that's become clearer to me over time is that everyone suffers from imposter syndrome to some degree, at some point in their lives. It's easy for us to doubt ourselves and wonder if what we have to say matters or even if it's worth saying in the first place. Find yourself a coach who will be straight with you and tell you if your communications are on-point or not. This third-party feedback is invaluable because you'll start to trust your own instincts more and realize that you *do* know what you're doing.

Chapter 7
Simplify to engagify

Of all the body's organs, the brain consumes the most energy. Though it accounts for only 2% of your body weight, it consumes 20% of your body's energy. In this regard, it is similar to your home's air conditioner—a relatively small appliance but a major consumer of power.

Burning calories means that your audience may be spending unnecessary mental energy to understand the content you're trying to convey. If the brain thinks it will have to spend too much energy processing the data it's confronted with, it will tune out and save that energy in case it is needed for survival.

People *pay* attention—quite literally—with the calories they use to process information.

We've all been there—that moment when someone's eyes glaze over, and it's obvious that we've lost them. They zone out and get lost in their own thoughts. When this happens, we're wasting our breath continuing speaking because they are no longer with us. We've lost engagement.

We've all seen an email that is TLDR (Too Long Didn't Read) or a presentation that is far too technical—a presentation that includes complex charts and slides that some might consider an eye chart because of the number of small typeface words that are on each slide.

The world isn't getting any simpler either. Technology has made our lives easier in many ways, but anyone who's had frustrations troubleshooting computers and consumer electronics knows how complicated things can get.

To ensure that your audience doesn't tune out, you need to simplify the message into consumable chunks that don't overwhelm the cognitive brain.

"Simplicity is the ultimate sophistication." This quote is often accredited to Steve Jobs, but it was actually uttered nearly 500 years ago by the original Renaissance man, Leonardo da Vinci. In our training sessions at *Engagify*, we teach subject matter experts how to be more engaging and present information in a compelling and connected manner. One of the challenges we face most often is when experts know too much and feel a compulsion to share every bit of that knowledge with the audience. Of course, knowledge isn't a bad thing, but the more you know, the more information you tend to try to communicate. This in turn overwhelms the audience and a clear, powerful, sophisticated message is lost.

From the perspective of any expert, simply stating basic information seems so obvious that he/she feels there needs to be more "meat" in the sandwich. In some cases, an expert may try to impress the audience with their intelligence and show off just how much they know. This is the kiss-of-death as it alienates the uninformed in the audience and possibly positions the speaker as a know-it-all.

Look smart by speaking simply enough that everyone understands

How do you know that everyone in the room can understand you? You can't know for certain, but if you choose to use a vocabulary that requires specialized knowledge, or if you make certain assumptions about how much your audience knows about your topic, you will lose some people because of these choices.

When clients hire our Certified Infotainers to draw crowds, create prospect engagement, and increase leads at trade shows, we customize the message for each client.

As outsiders, we are in a unique position. We ourselves must learn the company's value proposition and understand the core message that will be communicated in our trade show presentations. This means that if we can present the information in a way that *we* (as industry outsiders) understand it, then it follows that everyone will be able understand it. Give yourself the task of acting as a filter to sift out buzzwords, acronyms, and "new paradigms" in your message.

In 2016, I was working for a network security company in the North Hall of Moscone Center in San Francisco when a woman approached me after one of my presentations. She said, "I've been to all of these presentations and yours was the first I understood. You see, my husband brought me to this conference and I'm not in the industry."

If the outsider can understand you, then you leave no one behind. Frame your communication in such a way that everybody in attendance can follow along.

The curse of knowledge

Simplifying isn't easy, especially when you consider the corporate jargon that invariably finds its way into marketing and sales materials. Acronyms and buzzwords are common in the corporate setting, but these can mean multiple things to multiple people, or perhaps mean nothing at all to some. In a Forbes article, executive search consultant Michael Travis points out that, "*Aspiring managers would do well to remember that if you can't express your idea without buzzwords, there may not be an idea there at all.*"[1]

[1] M. Travis, *Annoying Business Jargon: 10 phrases entrepreneurs should avoid*, Forbes (2009). Available from www.forbes.com/2009/12/16/annoying-business-jargon-entrepreneurs-management-jargon_slide.html [accessed May 23, 2025].

The choice of words used is often to blame. Over time, every industry develops an "insider" language of acronyms and abbreviations that makes conversations more efficient for those in the know but virtually a foreign language to those who aren't in the same club. Experts in any given field should be wary of making content unnecessarily complicated.

When I was coaching trade show booth presenters for the European industrial manufacturing company Siemens, one of the presenters listed locations where solar power worked best. In his presentation, he used the term "areas of high solar radiation."

At this point, I interjected, "Do you mean the sunshine states?"

"Yeah," he replied.

"Then why don't you just say that?" I suggested.

It's amazing how we can find ourselves over complicating language just to sound smarter.

Acronyms are another area where we can lose people. When I'm forced to use acronyms in a trade show presentation for a client, I make it a practice to define the acronym before using it routinely. This brings outsiders into the loop so that no one is left behind.

Cognitive backlog, a phrase coined by Dr. Paul King of Texas Christian University, refers to the anxiety people feel when they get overloaded with a large amount of information in a short period of time. Burdened with the task of carrying too many facts and figures, the brain opts to lighten the load by dropping as much data as necessary. What this means for us in terms of engagement is that we need to reduce the amount of data and shorten our presentations so that a backlog doesn't build up.

A great example of conveying one big idea in a short, consumable presentation is a TED Talk. The 18-minute length is right in the "Goldilocks Zone" for attention spans.[2] Any longer and with

---

[2] C. Gallo, *Talk Like TED: The 9 public-speaking secrets of the world's top minds* (2014).

more detail, a presentation quickly becomes a case of diminishing returns so that length of time is considered just right.

When we consider all the trouble we go to to create a presentation or craft a story, it's disheartening to learn how little our audience actually remembers. According to Dr. Art Kohn, a researcher of cognitive science at Duke University, 50% of what we learn is forgotten within an hour, 70% within 24 hours and up to 90% just two days later. This means only 10% is remembered 48 hours after our presentation. With statistics this abysmal, it can make a person question why we bother sharing information at all.

The good news is there are things we can do to make our communications simpler and more memorable in order to increase retention and improve the impact of our message.

The fewer the better

Henry David Thoreau once said, "Simplify, simplify." In response to hearing this, his contemporary, Ralph Waldo Emerson, replied, "One 'simplify' would have sufficed."

People often assume that the relationship between choice and well-being must be straightforward. In other words, the more choices people have, the better. Ironically, according to Sheena Iyengar and Mark Lepper, publishing in the *Journal of Personality and Social Psychology*, this is not true.[3]

Their experiment, now known as the Jam Study, was conducted at the upscale supermarket Draeger's Market. One day, the store's customers were offered 24 different types of jam in the supermarket and, on the following day, customers were offered six types of jam. The researchers discovered a significant difference between the two cases—consumers were 10 times more likely to purchase jam

---

[3] S. S. Iyengar and M. R. Lepper, "When choice is demotivating: Can one desire too much of a good thing?" in *Journal of Personality and Social Psychology*, 79 (6), 995–1006 (2000). https://doi.org/10.1037/0022-3514.79.6.995.

on display when the number of types available was reduced from 24 to 6. In other words, the fewer the choices, the higher the sales.

The brains of the shoppers were overwhelmed with jam choices and found it easier to choose nothing than to make a decision about which jam to buy. Reducing the number of options we offer is a straightforward way to simplify. By reducing the number of points we make in a presentation, we increase the chances of our audience remembering our product or service. Simplified and remembered presentations decrease overwhelm and increase engagement.

The power of three

In experiments with short-term memory, scientists have discovered that we can only keep seven items (+/–2) in our conscious brain at one time—so, a maximum of nine and a minimum of five. It's no coincidence that most phone numbers are seven digits long.

What's simpler than the number five? Three! Three is a magical number. It's the lowest number you need to create a pattern. Consider storytelling ("The Three Little Pigs," "Goldilocks and the Three Bears"), comedy, and even the art of magic where the number three plays an important role in jokes and tricks.

One of the ways our company *Engagify* helps clients simplify their marketing messages for trade shows is to create a list of three well-known clients to be named in the presentation. This positions the company as a leader and legitimizes it in the marketplace. But our clients often have trouble narrowing down the list of candidates and want to have anywhere from four to seven names mentioned in our presentation. The problem is, the more information you give people, the less of it they will retain.

We instruct the client to choose only three, knowing that this improves uptake, retention—and also the meter and rhythm of the message as it's spoken. By mentioning only three items, and using **rhythm, rhyme, and repetition**, the message becomes stickier and more memorable.

As a case in point, consider the last sentence above. The idea I wanted to convey in that paragraph involves the concepts of cadence, rhyme, and alliteration. These are fine as individual concepts but aren't especially memorable as a group and lack punch. By making a few minor changes (*repetition* standing in for *alliteration* and *rhythm* for *cadence*) you get a much more memorable set of words.

The new triplet uses rhythm, rhyme, and repetition!

Primacy and recency

The primacy and recency effect is the notion that the information at the beginning and at the end of a presentation will be the most memorable. Knowing this and combining it with the magic of three, only the middle idea risks being forgotten.

The phenomenon of remembering the initial and final bits of information was originally discovered via an experiment in which a list of random words was read aloud to test subjects; later, the subjects' recall was tested by asking them to repeat as many of the items as they could. Researchers eventually established that those items at the beginning of a set (speech, story, presentation, or list) are stored in long-term memory while the most recent are stored in short-term memory. Items in the middle fall into cracks between the two.

What does this mean for you? To get your point across, don't hide the meat of your message in the middle. Open and close strong, with the core of your message located in each bookend. This finding emphasizes the classic advice of "tell them what you are going to tell them, tell them, then tell them what you told them."

For your next presentation—whether it be for your department, a customer or even at a Toastmasters club—decide on just three points to make. No more, no less. Decide which two of those are most important and put one at the beginning and one at the end.

Analogies and metaphors

The brain likes shortcuts. To save calories when figuring things out, the brain relies on learning heuristics. Heuristics are mental shortcuts for solving problems in a quick way; metaphors and analogies are two of the most popular kind. We love making connections and relating information to what we already know. Bolting new ideas onto accepted concepts helps us learn new things more quickly.

To leverage this tendency, employ stories and analogies to help get a point across. Whenever possible, talk about your solution in terms that are understandable and relatable. For example, at *Engagify*, we have been called "Red Bull for Sales Enablement." One of our clients who does asynchronous data replication refers to their disaster recovery solution as a "PVR (personal video recorder) for your data," conveying the idea that a user can rewind back in time to any point during the last two weeks.

In summary, consider:

▶ Replacing jargon and acronyms with common, relatable words.

▶ Reducing the number of chunks in your presentation down to three. Put the points you really want remembered at positions one and three.

▶ Using a commonly known metaphor or example to symbolize what you want to communicate.

Chapter 8
Go with the flow

There are those people who struggle every moment because things aren't perfect, and then there are those people who go with the flow and move through life with grace and poise.

Embracing the current moment instead of fighting it positions you as a confident leader. We all want to look to people who are cool under pressure and can be that steady hand on the wheel.

As humans, we have a need to "know." Uncertainty causes stress. Occasionally, I perform magic for smaller groups of people and every so often the group includes one of these "must know" types. They'll do anything to figure out how a trick is done because they hate not knowing. I've had people go so far as to put their hands in my pockets in search of the secret to a trick I've performed. However, once someone "knows" the secret behind the trick, they are often disappointed. Like a magic show, life is better enjoyed when we can accept things as they come and be fine with not knowing.

In the world of improv, not knowing what's going to happen is central to the art form. From moment to moment, you are experiencing the scene for the first time with your fellow improvisers. Your mind grasps for the next bit of information to help it all make sense. You're on stage without any apparent structure, exploring an idea or suggestion given by the audience. No lines, no set, no choreography, not even any defined beginning characters.

Notice I said there's no *apparent* structure. That's because there is actually a kind of structure or set of guidelines that helps facilitate the improvisation. The first and most important rule is to say "yes" to everything. This simple rule exists so that when someone introduces a reality to set the scene and denote character relationships, continuity can be built and the scene has a chance to develop. If a participant enters a scene and negates the existence of something that's already been established, it's called "blocking." Blocking is the opposite of saying "yes" or accepting the reality of what's being created. You can imagine how terrible a scene would be if an improviser didn't "go with it" and decided to shut down every new idea and piece of information that was introduced.

However, it's not enough to just say yes—the true rule is called: "Yes *and...*" This tiny but significant difference entails taking a suggestion from other improvisers and *adding* additional information and ideas to drive the plot forward and flush out the reality that is unfolding in the scene. Using "Yes and..." forces the improviser to accept the situation and go even further with it. When this rule is applied in a scene, a multitude of possibilities begin to emerge, making it easier for participants to keep the scene going and create on-the-spot theater.

When you think of improv, the famous Second City Theater probably comes to mind. One of the most famous improvisers to come out of Chicago's Second City is none other than Bill Murray. If you've ever watched old *Saturday Night Live* episodes or seen such classic movies as *Caddy Shack*, *Ghostbusters*, or *Groundhog Day*, you're well aware of Bill Murray's acting and comedic talents. His amazing improv skills aren't just reserved for the stage. Bill applies the "Yes and..." rule to his personal life to create unforgettable interactions that rise to legendary status.

A 2018 documentary film called *The Bill Murray Stories* explored and investigated some of the wild accounts of Bill Murray sightings that are often assumed to be urban legend. Whether it be singing karaoke late at night when Bill Murray joins the group, or being in a pub one night where Bill Murray starts bartending, each of the stories follows a familiar pattern: Normal, everyday people just doing their thing when in walks Bill Murray, who then embraces the situation and creates an unforgettable experience for everyone involved.[1] In one story, Murray was in the kitchen of a house party in Scotland doing the dishes. (There are many more stories just like this—I encourage you to Google "Bill Murray sightings" for more examples.)

The take-away from Mr. Murray's adventures is that he is open to experiencing all things in life. He engages life and is willing to see where things take him because he knows it won't just be memorable for him but for everyone involved. He takes the rules of improv to the highest level.

In my own life, I've incorporated this concept into my own performances. In my early twenties, I did my fair share of street performing. This involved finding a "pitch" or performance area that had enough walk-by traffic to enable the formation of my "edge" (the first row of audience members). The goal of course, was to build a crowd as large as possible, maximizing the income potential for when it came time to pass the hat at the end of the show.

Street theater, as it's also known, takes place outdoors in unconventional settings and is bound to have its share of distractions and challenges. This is no place to perform if you're a perfectionist. Nothing is going to happen exactly the way you plan it. You must embrace the chaos and instead of fighting it, feed off of it.

---

[1] T. Avallone (Director), *The Bill Murray Stories: Life lessons learned from a mythical man* [Film] (2018). www.imdb.com/title/tt7329810/

I did a fair bit of street performing in Manitoba at the Riding Mountain National Park. At the time, street performing was illegal, but I'd never had any issues with enforcement agencies when I performed my show on summer weekends. My pitch was in the downtown portion of the park's little resort town, on a piece of lawn in front of a museum and across from a street lined with shops and restaurants.

I'd plug in my sound system, start playing some music, and make a bit of a scene by cracking my whip and doing some machete juggling. Before long, some passing tourists would take notice and plant themselves on the grass in front of me with their ice cream cones, ready to be entertained. The more fun we had and the more noise we'd make, the bigger the crowd would get.

On one occasion, the local police parked their car across the street from where I had set up. I recall being kind of nervous, knowing that they were watching. I explained to my audience that the show might be cut short at any moment because of some "park rules" that I may be breaking.

The police, from inside their parked car, yelled over, "What are you doing over there with the whip and machetes?"

"Oh, just a little show I'm doing. Is there a problem, officer?" I said over the mic. Now, I could have packed up my show and ended it there, but from the tone of his voice it sounded a little playful.

"Are you supposed to be doing shows there?"

"I'm just sharing my talents with these fine people! Everyone— wave at the nice officers!" The crowd followed my lead and obliged my request.

Suddenly the lights on top of the police car flash on and everyone—including me—thought the show was as good as over. The car pulled away and over the loudspeaker we heard, "Have a good show!"

We all breathed a collective sigh of relief and continued the show with a new sense of community—bonded together by the common experience of uncertainty and not knowing what was going to happen next.

This short-lived quasi-confrontation created tension in the show as everyone held their breath, waiting to find out what would happen next. By choosing to just go with it and offering up a "yes and" with the crowd wave, we created a moment of playfulness that the police officers rewarded with a flash of their lights and the use of the loudspeaker. We served up the ball, and they returned our volley!

Interactions that are unrehearsed and in the moment are always the best kind. They're memorable and make for the best stories. When something out of the ordinary happens and you can say, "I was glad I was there for that!" everyone involved remembers the interaction. These ultra memorable events are rarely created through planning and choreography. It's the authenticity of the moment and the realness of the moment that brings it all together.

Engagify helps companies make their people and events more engaging. Sometimes, we're brought in to help make webinars more interesting and memorable. Often, we see webinar presenters who straight-up read their notes when giving presentations. While this can be perceived as professional and "on-point," it's far from engaging. No one wants to be *read* a presentation; we want to *experience* a presentation. These presenters are too busy clinging to their scripts instead of letting the moment present itself to them. They haven't yet learned to trust themselves under fire.

If you consider social media platforms like Facebook and LinkedIn, their "live" streams get more likes and comments than pre-recorded videos. This increased level of engagement is in part because live videos offer the chance for viewers to interact. The presenter in a live stream might answer viewer questions on the fly or mention a viewer's name out loud. The chances of going off-script are high because a great number of these live streams are very off-the-cuff. There's something irresistible about watching this type of content. There's a danger in it, a little like watching a high-wire act. You want to see the performer succeed and make it across safely, but at the same time, you enjoy watching the drama as they do so.

When a presentation is canned or pre-recorded, it removes much of the drama; in fact, some say a presentation can be too polished—a conclusion I've come to in my own trade show presentations. After several years of presenting, I realized there were two versions of a show competing in my mind. There was the scripted, planned, and rehearsed presentation—and there was the one that the audience needed in the moment.

The presentation that's planned and rehearsed is the one our clients hire us for. They want it to be "on-point," sharp, and focused on the elements they consider important. The intended presentation is free of distractions, snags and—many times—interactions. The performer doesn't diverge from the rehearsed scripted version, nor do they recognize or acknowledge the people standing in front of them. The performance would be the same with or without the audience, as the presenter ignores everything else that happens and goes on with the show. This is the type of delivery I'd want for a promo video, on-point and neutral.

However, the show the audience *needs* recognizes that each one of them is an individual. It acknowledges the environment and all the distractions that may come along. It means making use of "what is", being in the moment and completely alive. This kind of performance shows your audience that you are present, aware, and in tune with everything that's going on.

I used to fight to keep my performances "clean" of asides—personal references and ad-libs. But the more I performed, the more I came to realize that this type of show was sterile. It didn't hold the audience's attention. Incorporating elements that are of-the-moment is necessary to stamp the event into the minds of the audience and mark it as special and memorable.

Sticking to your routine of how you interact with people can become very predictable. Changing the arc of the conversation and interrupting the expected pattern by building on what an audience gives you can take you to very interesting and memorable places. So be more spontaneous, say "yes and" more often, and see where this takes you. You may find that people like being with you more. People might see time spent with you as more of an adventure.

Trust yourself and abandon perfectionism

The first step in bringing more spontaneity to your interactions is to be willing to trust yourself. You do this the same way a child learns to ride a bike: start with training wheels. You're going to have support at first—your notes, cheat sheets, whatever you need to be comfortable. Then slowly start experimenting, relying less on those supporting training wheels. They might still be handy, just don't use them every time. Find a low-risk situation where you can experiment without fear.

As you practice, you gain experience and expertise. With this competence, you build confidence. With confidence, you develop trust in yourself. There's a saying in farming that comes to mind: "All the hay is in the barn." Once you've done your work and paid your dues, you can relax and let the moment happen; you have the ability and now you just have to trust yourself.

Recognize that perfection is unattainable. We can strive for perfection but will very rarely achieve it. Embrace this concept and use it to your advantage. Don't fight the current, swim with it. Speaker and professional meeting summarizer Paul Huschilt says, "Perfection is death." Perfection is boring and gives you nothing to work with. I think about this whenever I see street performer play a soft seat theater. So much of a street performer's show revolves around interacting with passersby and gathering a crowd that when they already have a crowd seated and ready for a performance—they have very little material to perform. The lack of distractions in the theater removes the potential for suggestions that the performer can accept and develop.

In improv you can't force your agenda—you have to be open to the contributions of your fellow improvisers. Let go and observe with a keen sense of curiosity. Abandoning the pursuit of perfection allows you to be more detached from the outcome and enables you to have a sense of play. In your play, you may discover a perfect off-the-cuff line, one that only came to you because you weren't rigidly attached to your script. This line, question, or "bit" can be reused in similar situations, but it will never be as perfect as the first time you used it.

You may have seen old school performers who've used the same schtick forever—they get stuck in a rut, doing the same thing over and over again. Their act gets predictable and stale.

Just like improvisers, whatever the moment gives you, take the suggestion and build on it. Look at everything coming at you as a gift. Accept it, use it, and see what you can make of it. Be detached from the outcome and embrace the chaos. You'll be more engaging and memorable because of it.

Chapter 9
When you're smiling

When we see someone we would like to greet or engage with, what is the first thing we do? As we approach someone, we display a signal that communicates that we are non-aggressive and that we come in peace. That signal, of course, is a smile.

If you have children, nothing quite compares to the first time you ever see your child smile. Chances are they're just passing gas that first time, but it doesn't change the way you feel inside. That smile is one of the first indications as to what might be going on inside that little head of theirs. It lights you up inside, and you realize how much joy such a small facial expression can bring.

A smile is more than just an expression of happiness—it's also an invitation to others to engage. A smile signals approachability. Scientists believe that the smile was born out of the need for primates to show others that they meant no harm. When two apes meet face to face in the wild, there's the risk of confrontation. A smile diffuses tension and sends the message that you come in peace and that you are non-threatening.

With our busy lives and everyday stresses, we don't often think about the messages we send with our facial expressions and body language. We're so preoccupied with our internal thoughts that we forget how we are being perceived and how that affects the quality and quantity of our interactions.

Back when I performed at corporate events, I was continuously reminded of this. In the middle of my show, I would spot the event planner, who would have a concerned look on their face. Immediately I would second-guess how I was doing because my client didn't appear to be amused with the performance. After the show I would check in with the planner, and the feedback was always positive. If I ever mentioned that they didn't seem to be enjoying themselves, they would admit that they were probably thinking about the logistics and timing of the rest of the event.

We're influenced by body language to a much greater degree than we think, but the reality is, millions of years of evolutionary programming guide our actions. Even subtle, seemingly insignificant gestures can make or break the moment. Auctioneers in auctioneer school (yes, that's a thing) are taught to move their hand in a "come here" motion as they chant. These hand gestures are intended to invite bids. They are also taught not to hold up their hands with their palms facing outward (in a stopping motion), as that would slow down the action.

To engage our audiences, our prospects, and clients, we have to be holding the door open so they can walk through effortlessly. We need to eliminate barriers that can unconsciously deter people from entering into an engagement.

When it comes to approachability, no one has taken things farther than Scott Ginsberg. After attending an event where the classic "Hi, my name is…" nametag stickers were being used, he decided to keep his nametag on after the event, just for fun. He met 20 new people that first day. As an experiment, he continued to wear the nametag (likely replacing it occasionally as the stickiness wore off). At the time of this writing, his nametag streak is 7500 consecutive days and counting. (He didn't let moments of shirtless-ness hold him back in his quest for engagement—he had the "nametag" tattooed on his chest.)

What he found was that the nametag broke the ice and gave people a reason to say hello. He admits that he receives many of the same comments: "Do you have a bad memory?" or "Do you know you're still wearing your nametag?" One of his favorite comments came from a big burly bouncer outside an Irish pub who said, "We don't allow 'Scotts'!" In spite of all the reoccurring comments, Ginsberg finds wearing the nametag is worthwhile for the opportunities and interactions it creates.

While living in Portland and writing his first book, a stranger struck up a conversation with Ginsberg on the bus. Scott mentioned his upcoming book and the stranger asked for his business card. A week later, Ginsberg was called by the *Portland Tribune*, which ran a four-page feature article about his yet-to-be released book. The article was syndicated all over the U.S. and resulted in a guest appearance on CNN. How did all of this happen to a guy whose book wasn't even out yet? The stranger on the bus that day was the fiancée of the editor of the *Portland Tribune*.

The nametag created the interaction, which then led to a PR opportunity worth hundreds of thousands of dollars. The question is, how many strangers are you avoiding and how many opportunities are you missing out on?

For 20 years, Scott Ginsburg has been wearing a nametag— which has led to the creation of his personal brand. He's famous for doing something that anyone could do, but didn't. Over the past two decades, he's written 50 books and become an expert in approachability and personal branding. Ginsburg is convinced that we all have the potential to be more approachable and to find our own nametag in life.

I'm not saying you should wear a nametag to be approachable and engaging—there are other, more subtle ways of sending the right message. But what we need to recognize is that our actions and the energy we send out into the world are our nametags. We send a message to those around us about who we are by the way we move, the way we dress, and the energy we give off. The significance of the metaphorical nametag is that we have confidence in our own unique identities. When we proudly give ourselves to the world, we become approachable, welcoming, and more interesting because of it.

Approachability is very much linked to the level of comfort we have in our own skins. I like to run to clear my mind and get some exercise, and I've noticed something about other people who run. If you've been a runner for some time, maybe you've noticed that there's a secret code of sorts. When you pass another runner going the opposite way, you both smile and nod in a mutually respectful way that acknowledges the other's commitment to their health and says, "Good on ya!"

When you lead with a smile and someone doesn't look or give you the time of day, you immediately form an opinion of that person. You're left wondering, "What's their problem?" If my smile isn't returned, or even acknowledged, it may be because this runner is someone who isn't comfortable with being a runner or maybe they're just beginning their "health journey" and are focused on their process or managing pain. Maybe they aren't quite sure if they belong in the club and they keep to themselves. Regardless of their reasoning behind their sober expression, they may be surprised that if they would only look, they would see the smile and nod that might be the slap on the back they need for being out there and exercising.

As mentioned previously, the smile or "fear grin" was posited as a defense mechanism that primates developed to show that they meant no harm. Over time, the smile has evolved to become a symbol of many things: happiness, joy, warmth, laughter, comedy, and so on. Because smiles are so deeply seated in our wiring, their significance goes beyond the visual indication. Humans can even hear it in a smile.

In 2008, scientists in the United Kingdom found that people don't have to see a smile to perceive one.[1] Not only can we detect

---

[1] P. M. Niedenthal and M. Brauer, "The role of facial feedback in emotion perception: A review of the literature" in *Emotion*, 12 (1), 92–105 (2012).

the existence of a smile through the sound of a voice, but we can detect which kind of smile it is. The tightening of the lips or the "smile effect" can be registered on an unconscious level, and just as when we see a smile, hearing a smile also induces smiling in the recipient. It seems we tend to mirror what we hear as well as what we see.

In addition, a smile can create a "wag the dog" effect—meaning that we smile when we're happy, and when we smile, it can positively affect our mood. The same is true of frowning. Scientists found an off-label treatment for depression using Botox—a drug injected into the face to paralyze muscles and prevent permanent frown lines. What they found was that the Botox prevented patients from frowning deeply with their brows, and patients reported having lighter moods because of it.

All this means that our smiles—even when they can't be seen—can influence our audiences by changing their states, breaking down barriers, and creating connection. Our approachability can have a butterfly effect on those around us, creating the possibility of increased interactions and engagement.

As humans, we are constantly scanning the environment around us for potential threats. We have an uncanny knack for analyzing facial expressions so that we can be more empathetic. Back in the 1980s, Anne Treisman and Garry Gelade proved that subjects were faster at locating a face among non-face objects. They proved that faces naturally capture attention. The human face has been proven to be the most stimulating 3D object we can observe. Little wonder we experience "Zoom fatigue," looking at all of our co-workers' constantly changing expressions in the gallery view. Because we are constantly on the lookout for threats, seeing a smile relaxes us because we immediately understand, in a broad sense, the mental state of our counterpart. A smile is reassuring and indicates no harm.

This also applies to pictures of faces, even as small as an emoji. Alek Chakroff and Adam Anderson examined the effect of emojis on the brain compared to real human faces.[2] It turns out that an emoji stimulated the same brain regions as face procession. If you want to communicate nuances and tone in your writing, don't be afraid to use an emoji. They're not just for teenagers. 😊

So, if you're a person who's known to come off as cold or even rude, or you just want to up your approachability index, here are some ways of becoming more approachable so you can invite engagement.

Smile

The first strategy to become more approachable is to remember to smile. Before there were virtual calls, sales experts used to recommend you keep a mirror by the phone so that you could see your facial expressions as you spoke. This mirror not only reminded you to smile, it also provides visual feedback on how you are being perceived.

Today, we spend much of our time communicating on virtual calls. While some may not want to see themselves on screen, it is highly recommended that you get real-time feedback on the messages you are sending out to the world. Over time, you will find yourself developing a habit of naturally smiling when required.

When you smile, make it a Duchenne smile. Scientists have defined up to 19 different kinds of smiles, yet only two main types have been identified as being the most important. The Duchenne smile and the non-Duchenne smile. The Duchenne smile is named after the 18th-century scientist, Guillaume Duchenne, who mapped the facial muscles. A Duchenne smile is a true, authentic smile that signifies true enjoyment. It occurs when the facial muscle zygomaticus major lifts the corners of the mouth and the orbicularis oculi muscles lift your cheeks and makes your

---

[2] A. Treisman and G. Gelade, "A feature-integration theory of attention" in *Cognitive Psychology*, 12 (1), 97–136 (1980). www.sciencedirect.com/science/article/abs/pii/0010028580900055?via%3Dihub

eyes crinkle at the corners. Not everybody likes to have crow's feet or smile lines, but those come from real authentic smiles.

Non-Duchenne smiles are half smiles or fake smiles. These are smiles that are "put-on" and they come off as insincere and phony. While any smile is better than no smile at all, in order to create a smile with a twinkle in your eye, be sincere and show them your pearly whites!

Stand out

This next tip sounds like something you might find on a dating site, but it works in the business arena as well. Whether it's wearing a "Hello, My Name Is" nametag, sporting a bowtie, carrying an umbrella as an accessory, or wearing a piece of statement jewelry, do wear something that is out of the ordinary to invite conversation. As a trade show presenter, I wear a suit and always choose a tie that matches the color of my client's branding. Sometimes this means wearing a tie in an unusual color you might not expect to see— namely fuchsia pink, neon green, or solid white. Whenever I wear these coordinating ties, I get comments from people proclaiming their appreciation of the tie.

Stand up and open

Sometimes being more approachable means being cognizant of your body language. Crossing your arms or holding your hands in front of you can make you appear closed off. When teaching trade show booth staff how to work a trade show exhibit, we emphasize the importance of open body language to invite interested prospects more effectively (not unlike the auctioneer example we mentioned earlier). Keeping your head up and your body angled towards people also encourages others to interact with you.

Additionally, watch the feet. When someone's feet are pointing away from you while you are engaged in a conversation, it infers they are ready to leave. Just make sure that as you're observing and analyzing the body language of your conversational partner, to ensure you aren't sending the wrong signals with your own body—point your feet at the person you're speaking with and engage them head on.

Speak outrageously

Use flavored answers when someone asks you a question. What's a flavored answer, you might ask? It's an unexpected answer that takes a person by surprise and underlines your answer. Instead of saying "Yes," try saying "Absolutely." Absolutely is such an overwhelmingly positive response that it affirms the other person for asking the question.

Instead of answering "Fine" when asked "How are you?", try using "Remarkable!" or "If I was any better, I'd be two people!" Answers that stray from the norm create curiosity and often lead to more questions. An enthusiastic response coaxes the other party to join the interaction. It also shows that you aren't threatening and that you like to have fun—both qualities that will serve you in welcoming engagement.

To create a memorable interaction with someone, being approachable is key. Welcoming them into a situation using a smile and other techniques listed here, will get the ball rolling. The old Louis Armstrong lyrics ring true: "When you are smiling, the whole world smiles with you."

Chapter 10
Storytelling: the master-skill

Why are stories so engaging? The structure of a good story is designed to suck us in and makes us pay attention. We have no choice—we're wired to find stories compelling and the better the story and the better the storyteller, the more engaged we will be.

The art of storytelling dates to early man, when cavemen related their great hunting feats to others around the fire. Good stories are the perfect vehicle for passing down oral history to younger generations because they are memorable.

Part of why stories are so memorable and engaging is that we see ourselves in them. When a scene is set and the conflict is introduced, we can't help imagining ourselves in the same position. Our empathic tendencies kick in and we start experiencing the same feelings as the story's protagonist. We tend to remember things better when we visualize them, so the more vividly we imagine a story in our minds, the more memorable it will be. This active participation in the story (imagining it as it's being described) really is the characterization of engagement—being actively involved in something.

It's not just your imagination that makes stories work—it's the structure of the story itself. All good stories have a basic structure that can be rudimentarily summarized as follows: a monkey runs up a tree, you throw rocks at the monkey, and then you get the monkey off the tree. The ideas of character, conflict, and triumph are essential to every story. This idea of *The Hero's Journey* was developed by Joseph Campbell and explored in his book *The Hero with a Thousand Faces*.[1] For those unfamiliar with Joseph Campbell, he studied great stories from around the world and was able to distil them down to a formula that you can see play out in all movies—from *Star Wars* to *Jerry Maguire*. This formula never fails to please.

Now you might be thinking, "I'm not a George Lucas or a Mark Twain—what do I do?" Fear not, because all stories need not be Tom Sawyer.

When I was a young magician in middle school, I read that Harry Houdini was a teetotaler, so I decided to follow in his footsteps and chose not to drink alcohol. This meant that later on, as a university student, I was usually the only one not drinking in the bar. The way I made myself feel accepted and at home was to perform magic and entertain people at the club. This was my go-to move to help me feel comfortable in a group. My repertoire included card tricks, cigarette tricks, and even "watch steals," in which I'd rob someone's wrist of their timepiece and present it back to them as a gift, or transpose it on to my accomplice's wrist.

One evening at my best friend's law school graduation, I found myself entertaining his classmates at a swanky private club. At the time, I was really into stealing watches—ever since stealing my first leather strap watch from an old lady at a fair, I'd been hooked. I got a huge rush from taking a watch from someone's wrist, right under their nose, without being detected. After a while, I had to steal more and more challenging watches in order to get the same rush. The most difficult watches to steal were the timepieces with

---

[1] J. Campbell, *The Hero with a Thousand Faces* (1949).

expandable bracelets with clasps to prevent accidental opening like the Oysterlock safety clasp you'd see on a diving watch like a Rolex Submariner. This style had to come off the wrist and down over the hand, instead of simply falling off the wrist once the clasp was opened.

On this particular night, I spotted an expandable bracelet watch on one of my spectator's wrists. The guy was 6' 4" and solidly built. I mention his size because his hands were very large, which meant that the watch would be a lot tougher to slide over his hand without him knowing.

Before I continue, I should mention that stealing watches—and pick-pocketing in general—is a risky style of magic. If you get caught red-handed, there's no out. There's no Plan B. The effect is blown and you must retreat with your tail between your legs. Not only that, but there's always the risk that someone may not understand that you're doing this to entertain and not to actually steal the watch, which can result in a pretty unpleasant scene— especially if the watch is a pricey one, like it was in this particular instance.

I began with a coin routine, which acted as a guise to get me close to my subject and gave me an excuse to touch his wrist. I explained to him how the coin was going to jump from one of his hands to the other. I had carefully positioned his watch hand in such a way that his thumb was tucked in to facilitate easier removal of the watch. His right hand was carefully positioned in the area where the coin "magic" was to take place, shielding his view of the dirty work that was about to happen to his other wrist below.

I secretly undid the clasp and had the watch open and hanging loosely on his wrist. I now had to maneuver the watch down towards his fingers. The hardest part of stealing this type of watch is hitting the point of no return. This is the point where the hand is widest and the watch gets really snug. When you've reached this point, the next move is the riskiest step of the whole trick. You basically rip the watch off and pray that they don't notice. In reality, it's a little more nuanced than that because your patter (the words you say and the story you tell) and body language create misdirection, hopefully covering the fact that you just ripped a watch off the other person's hand.

On this man, the watch was snug and I knew I'd have to yank hard. Now, understand that to *him* the trick hadn't even begun, yet I had almost done the dirty work. The fact that the watch was snugger than usual did give me pause. There was a good chance I could get caught stealing this watch, which would be embarrassing, but there's no way I could just bail in the middle of a trick and lose all the momentum I'd created. With that in mind I gave the watch a solid yank, exclaimed that the coin had transposed and commanded him to look in his non-watch hand.

I had created a habit of looking someone dead in the eyes right after I performed a watch steal. It was the moment of truth. Did I get away with it? Did they know I took their watch? Are they going to play along or are they mad I've taken their watch? If so, how mad? Are they going to take a swing at me?

His expression was confused, as the coin hadn't materialized as I'd promised (even though it never would). He was still inside the reality that I had created and oblivious to what had just taken place. As a magician, your job is to misdirect and lead a person's attention away from the secret of the trick and not point out what's about to happen. When stealing watches, you should never cast your gaze onto the left wrist from which you just stole the watch. The audience (and your watch steal victim) will always look where you look, and you don't want to give away what has just transpired. But in this instance, because of how tight the watch was on the widest part of his hand, I broke this rule and took a quick look.

I could see white bits of scraped skin on his hand where the watch had scratched. At that moment, I realized that if I were able to complete this trick it would be nothing short of a miracle. Not only did I take his watch without his noticing, I inflicted pain on him while doing so. This is not a judgment of this man and his self-awareness—it's a testament to the power of a story and the focus we put on that story. I had painted a picture of the miracle that was going to happen with the coins in his hand, and he was so invested in that story that he blocked out all other distractions—including the scraping of his wrist.

Stories focus the imagination on something and engage the mind in ways that nothing else can. If you want to hold focus, command attention, and be remembered—you must start telling stories.

My high school science teacher knew this and used the phenomenon to great effect. Whenever he felt the class energy waning, he would say, "Time for a story!" and the class would perk up. As students, we knew this meant we could rest our minds and just listen and take a much-needed break.

Stories play to the right side of our brains—the side that is creative, imaginative, artistic. The left side is associated with logic, structure, language, and so on. Stories are a powerful tool for dealing with overly analytical people. In sales situations you may sometimes be confronted with someone who seems intent on tearing apart your product, process, or service every chance they get. When you run into someone who has this analytical framework, tell them a story of a past client, or maybe a story from your childhood that acts as a metaphor for the key point you're trying to make. The story will take them out of their left brain and put them into their "right mind," which can clear the way for you and make your sale easier.

Now, some of you may be experiencing an unconscious nagging sensation right now—a slightly unsettled feeling arising from the lack of closure to my story. You might even be annoyed with me, as the storyteller, because I have left you hanging. Are you wondering if the man was surprised when I handed his watch back to him? Whether he was mad? How it all ended?

I pulled the watch from my pocket and, knowing the value of his own watch, his jaw hit the floor and his hand instantly went to his wrist. The crowd erupted and his buddies razzed him for the rest of the night for losing his watch. Once things settled down,

I pointed out to him that his hand was scraped and red from my stealing maneuver, and we had a good laugh! Luckily, things went as planned and it was a great finale for my impromptu magic performance. Nothing beats a watch steal for a big reaction.

Now that I've finished the story, do you feel better? You've just experienced what scientists call the Ovsiankina Effect.[2] Named after the researcher Maria Ovsiankina, it states that an unfinished task creates intrusive thoughts that demand closure of that task. You may have also experienced this if you've ever started watching a movie during a flight and then landed at your destination before you were able to finish it. There's a certain feeling that hangs with you for a while; it's usually remedied on the return flight when you can pick up where you left off.

Stories have a beginning, middle, and end and we know this intuitively. So when a story is interrupted or left unfinished, we become very attentive to the storyteller as we don't want to miss the ending. This need for closure is sometimes called a story loop. By introducing a problem, a story loop is created, and the spectator wants to see the problem resolved. In my trade show performances, I state that someone in the audience will have a chance to win the fan of twenty $100 bills that I'm holding. This opens a loop that demands closure. People will stay for 30 minutes to see if they'll win the $2000 cash and if not them, if someone else will. This lack of resolution is a hard thing to walk away from. We need closure so we stay for the ending.

Consider the magic illusion in which a person is made to disappear and then brought back. The trick/story isn't complete until everything is resolved. Both of these above instances are examples of piquing someone's curiosity and opening a story loop—a loop that won't be closed until the story is complete.

When I was training to work trade shows, my mentor said that I would forget 90% of the information from the training, but

[2] M. Ovsiankina, "Die Wiederaufnahme unterbrochener Handlungen" in *Psychologische Forschung*, 11, 302–379 (1928).

I would remember all of the stories. He was right. Fifteen years later, I still remember the lessons from the stories and even the story plots themselves. If you want your message to be remembered, tell a story that backs up your point. Take this book, for example— each chapter has a small story to help engage your right mind and hammer home the point of the chapter.

Becoming a better storyteller

So, we know that stories can create focus, keep people's attention and make your content more memorable. But how do we become better storytellers?

The first thing you need to know is that you don't need to have scaled Mount Everest or overcome perilous odds to have a great story. Stories are everywhere—you just have to tune your attention to them. To become a storyteller, you must become a story collector.

Get yourself a nice Moleskine notebook, or something that you'll take pride writing in. Then, just start writing down things that have happened to you. They don't have to be full-fledged stories at this point, just story ideas. Once you start writing, more and more stories are going to come to you. It's a classic example of whatever you focus on, you get more of. Kind of like the car you're considering buying and suddenly you start seeing everywhere— once you start collecting stories, you'll see potential for stories everywhere.

Next, go through your list and write out a story in long form. By taking the time to structure the story, you'll better understand which parts are necessary for the story to come together. Writing and rewriting will crystalize the plot and make it memorable for you.

Then I recommend creating a story index or database. This can be in your notebook or an Excel spreadsheet, if you prefer. This is your quick reference guide. Create columns for story name, characters, lesson learned, basic plot and any other data points you'd like to track. This will be helpful when it comes time to choose a story for a specific presentation or speech.

Depending on how you spin a story, that same story can contain multiple lessons. For example, I sometimes use my Watch Steal Story to talk about risk versus reward or commitment and taking action. Your stories can become Swiss Army knives in the sense that only a few stories can serve you in a multitude of ways. In your story index, be sure to list all the possible lessons that can be learned from each story.

Once you have a few stories fully written, test them out. Don't choose a high-stakes meeting as the place to tell your story for the first time. Rather, pull out your story at a family dinner or a networking event. Practice it in a setting where you can learn from the crowd. By getting your story on its feet, you'll discover which parts are funny and which parts people love best. Just looking at their faces and noticing when they chuckle will give feedback on both your story and your storytelling technique.

Once you have a few repetitions of a story under your belt, you may want to rewrite things slightly and implement any changes you see fit. Then you can look for ways to tweak your delivery—changing your voice, acting out certain sequences, or playing it bigger, for example. I have a story about the first time I went waterskiing and lost my trunks—believe me, it cannot be told properly without some pantomime to truly paint the picture.

The skill of weaving a well-told story is the master-skill of engagement. Stories have such a significant impact on our imaginations that the ability to tell a good story is the great equalizer in the pursuit of engagement. You don't have to be charming or charismatic, because stories have the ability to do so much of the heavy lifting. By recognizing that we all have stories to tell, then working and practicing our stories, we can all become good storytellers.

PART 3
ADVANCED ENGAGEMENT

Chapter 11
Engaging personas

The word *persona* comes from the ancient Greek "persono" or "to sound through," in reference to the dramatic masks that actors would use to amplify their voices in the open-air amphitheaters. Now the term has come to mean a character or a social role.

We all wear different masks at different times and we tend to be different "characters" depending on the context. When I'm out with my guy friends, I'm different than when I'm with my wife. When I'm with my kids, I'm more animated and playful. We match the social context we're in to bring out the parts of ourselves that best serve the moment.

Examples of this can be also found in the fields of sports and entertainment. Beyoncé Knowles not only has an onstage persona, she has even given her a name—"Sasha Fierce." Beyoncé attributes part of the success she's achieved as a live performer to the confidence she receives from this alter ego. Sasha Fierce is a part of her that comes out when she is ready to take the stage and perform in front of her adoring fans. When interviewed by Oprah, Beyoncé said that Sasha Fierce emerges, "When I hear the chords and I put on my stilettos. I was nervous the moment right before… then Sasha Fierce appears and my posture and the way I speak is different."

Another example of this alternate persona concept is the late basketball great Kobe Bryant. He referred to his competitive on-court self as "The Black Mamba." He coined this nickname for himself while going through a slump in his career. To get into this ultra-competitive mindset, Kobe listened to the theme song from the movie *Halloween*. It took him to a place where he could be devoid of pressure and emotion—just like the character Mike Myers and the mask he wore in the movie—single-minded in his determination.

Kobe felt the persona helped him move out of his slump. "I'm destroying everybody that steps on the court. I had all this pent-up frustration that I needed to let out. It was an avalanche, man. There was nothing that was going to get in the way. There was nothing that was going to stop me."

These two examples might seem extreme, but they illustrate the lengths to which masters in their fields have gone to generate their desired results. The important take-away in the cases of Sasha Fierce and Black Mamba is that even the most famous and talented people in the world sometimes need a little extra boost to get the most out of themselves. If you consider yourself an introvert, shy or just not comfortable with putting yourself out there, this approach has some obvious applications that you may find useful. For those of you who love the spotlight and aren't afraid of taking risks, you may find it a good way of pushing yourself to new and greater heights.

I've experienced this in my own career. From the early days of performing at kids' birthday parties, to conferences and corporate events, I consciously recognized that I needed to be a pumped up version of myself. I wasn't trying to be someone different, just bringing an element of my personality to the forefront and amplifying it. The audience feedback helped me to dial in those parts of my behavior and I started to recognize where my "sweet spot" lies.

When I started performing at trade shows, I tried bringing that same persona to this new environment but found it difficult at first. For one, I was no longer dealing with a captive audience seated in a banquet hall with nowhere to go. My new audience was an aisle of transient attendees with things to do and appointments to keep.

In 2007, I trained with Joel Bauer, who is known in the magic world for being at the top of the food chain when it came to corporate work and specifically, trade shows. I spent four days listening to his language patterns and philosophies and watching him move with pure intention and congruence. To see him work a crowd—literally commanding the audience to do something and seeing them respond—was a thing to behold. His presence and confidence were off the charts and I knew that I wanted that level of influence. He, too, had evolved over time to create a performance persona that was more effective at engaging people in a high-distraction environment like a noisy trade show floor.

In order to land my first trade show client and to create a promo video, Joel gave me an intimidating assignment. He insisted that I find a trade show to "crash." This meant gaining access to a trade show (preferably for free) and going from booth to booth offering a free presentation that would integrate the company's marketing message and create a crowd of people around their booth.

The first trade show I ever crashed was a cyber security show in Toronto. *En route* to Toronto I was sick with dread at the thought of approaching companies cold and having the audacity to claim that I could put a crowd of people in their booth and work their value proposition into the show—all on the fly.

I got into the show effortlessly enough and took a walk around, checking out all the companies in attendance. I had no specific reason for doing this, just stalling and biding my time before making my first approach. I was so nervous I thought I might throw up. I found a quiet, out-of-the-way corner and called my wife for moral support. Knowing me like she does, she said all the right things and helped me to calm down and get focused. Finally, after stalling for most of the morning, I finally found the courage to approach exhibitors.

After approaching five companies I finally got a bite. But now I had to deliver on my promise. I had to start a presentation without an audience and build a crowd as quickly as possible while trying to shoe-horn customized messaging into a magic show that I had prepared. This wasn't something I'd done before and not something I was at all comfortable with. My heart pounded in my chest as the company's marketing manager and booth staff looked on, waiting for me to start.

What followed was not what I had expected. I started my routine and found myself talking and moving just like my mentor, Joel. It was as if I was channeling him as a means of bolstering my confidence and winning over and engaging passersby. Initially, it felt strange—this was not how I usually performed—but it was working. I was able to draw a decent-sized crowd and deliver on my promise to the company.

What I learned from that experience was exactly what Joel had told me all along. If I projected the right amount of confidence, the people would follow. I needed to use commanding tones and spoke with confidence. I had to **tell people** to move in, not ask politely. My body language was bigger than normal, with strong, decisive movements that gave a sense of urgency and conviction to the performance. These characteristics made the presentation intrinsically more interesting in order to compete with the distracting environment.

Different situations call for different parts of your personality to emerge—in some cases, parts you didn't even know you had. If you're looking to cultivate an engaging personality, you may need to stretch yourself in ways you never have before.

My colleague Dave Byrnes (not of the Talking Heads) speaks on being an introverted networker. We were both attending a virtual conference together, and the attendees were discussing the challenges of engaging online. The camera seems to kill your energy, so you need to increase your energy level so that you come across the way you intend to.

With a straight face and dry, sardonic sense of humor, he said, "You won't believe this, but I'm actually plugged into the sun right now." You see, for an introvert like Dave, just being on Zoom and knowing that people were watching, required a great deal of energy and concentration to just to be on the call.

Eventually in my own work, I became comfortable bringing this new level of energy to my trade show performances. I kept the new performance characteristics that worked for me and integrated them into my performance persona.

Whether you are an extravert, introvert or ambivert, or you just have trouble reaching out and connecting with people, there is a way to go about doing it successfully. It may not be comfortable at first, but if you are willing to experiment, you may find you can tease out a part of yourself that you didn't know existed.

Here are two ideas to help you discover that engaging persona within you.

Be intentional

Be aware of how you move. Most of us move through life in a way that Zig Ziglar described as "wandering generalities instead of meaningful specifics." We gesture half-heartedly—our movements are lazy and uninspired. The way we carry ourselves says more about our apathy for the message than the message itself.

When we put intention behind our movement, it gives greater meaning to our body language. It demands to be seen and communicates a more congruent message.

Congruence is the idea that your thoughts, words, and actions are in complete alignment. When these three factors align, your intention becomes clear and easily understood. The next time you have a mission-critical interaction planned—be it a sales meeting, a date, or an important presentation—enter into the interaction with a specific intention. Find a verb that you can "do." It might be to inspire, to motivate, to energize, to seduce, and so on. Try rehearsing the interaction and experiment with different intentions. Observe the way that it affects how you speak, how you act, and how you move. Watch how people respond and make a note of their reactions.

Play big

Play bigger in your interactions. Amy Cuddy, a social psychologist from Harvard Business School, found that taking up more physical space with your body actually changes your body chemistry, gives you a confident presence, and more perceived leadership qualities. She found that just three minutes in a power pose was enough to change the body chemistry and give you a boost in presentations, job interviews, and other key events.

I personally subscribe to the hands-on-hips (Wonder Woman) pose as my go-to when waiting to give a training or keynote. It's a far more resourceful state than being head down on my phone with my elbows tucked in. Own your space, play big, and give more of yourself to your interactions.

Create anchors

A performance hack that comes courtesy of neuro linguistic programming (NLP) is anchoring. An anchor is any stimulus that triggers a particular behavior. This Pavlovian response can be created to help bring us into a resourceful state. The stimulus can be just about anything—a piece of music that you listen to (Kobe Bryant), a piece of clothing that you wear (Beyoncé)—that instantly triggers you to become the person you need to be.

After years of performing in a suit, I found that once I suited up, I stood taller, walked more powerfully, and was ready to go to battle. My suit became an anchor that was triggered unconsciously because it was always a part of my pre-show process.

For the past few years, I have also used an olfactory anchor as a very intentional way of bringing about a certain state. The olfactory sense is the express train to the brain is an incredibly powerful tool for bringing back memories. We have scents that instantly take us back to our childhood when we smell them. One of mine is the smell of powdered Tide soap. Why? As a kid, I had a special box for my G.I. Joes that my mom made for me from an old Tide box.

To create an olfactory anchor for yourself, try an aromatherapy inhaler. It doesn't matter which aroma or essential oil you use, as long as the scent isn't a powerful, pre-existing reminder of something for you. To do this successfully, catch yourself in a peak state. Then, while you are "in the zone", smell your inhaler for the first time. Catch yourself in the zone a couple more times and repeat. Once you have set your anchor, you are ready to use it whenever you want to trigger your desired state.

Before I am about to start a presentation, I take a whiff up each nostril and suddenly there's a voice in my head saying, "Let me at 'em!" I feel bulletproof and ready to deliver whatever performance or presentation that is before me.

Try this for yourself and see if you can create a Black Mamba or Sasha Fierce of your own.

Chapter 12
Architecting ahas

Snail mail isn't as common as it used to be, as many companies have made the switch to email marketing. But for those of you who have ever received a lumpy mailer, I'm sure you remember what was inside. Lumpy mail is a tactic used in direct mail marketing to get envelopes opened and letters read. *Lumpy* refers to the thickness created by the inclusion of something in the envelope to arouse the recipient's curiosity. You'd feel the lump and wonder what's inside, and, of course, you would have to open it to satisfy your curiosity.

Inside is a small trinket. Maybe it's a tiny flashlight or perhaps a magnifying glass. Immediately you ask yourself, "Who would send you this... and why?" Then you see the headline on the sales letter which reads, "Let us shine some light on your lawn care problems" or "Let's take a closer look at the value of your home." Suddenly, the trinket makes sense and you experience a mini "aha" moment. You might think it's clever or you might think it's hokey, but either way, the letter got opened and the message was received.

Lumpy mailers are a gimmick to secure attention, and they work—even when you know the true intent behind them. This is true for a number of attention-seeking devices. You know what's happening, but you can't help yourself.

Our own presentations and interactions need an equivalent to the lumpy mailer—something to promote curiosity and use as a springboard to make your points interesting and memorable.

If you have never received a lumpy mailer, you may relate to your high school science teacher's demonstrations. I vividly remember walking into the science lab and seeing stands, rings and Bunsen burners set up on the bench at the head of the class. I'd be hooked instantly, wanting to know what was going to happen in class that day.

The same is true of watching a street performer setting up his equipment. Observing the various props that will be used during the performance, you can't help but wonder what the performer is going to do with all those machetes—and what's up with the bull whip??

These attention grabbers can take many shapes and forms. It might be a picture, an object, or a demonstration. It might be a story or a metaphor, it might even be a magic trick.

I've made a career out of combining magic and marketing by exploiting people's inherent fascination with magic and adding a relevant marketing message. My style of infotainment isn't for everyone. Some have called what I do gimmicky. I don't mind. In fact, the word gimmick is derived from the art of magic. It's a secret device or gadget that makes the trick work. The bottom line is—gimmicks are necessary for the magic to happen. If something is effective, don't judge it—use it and exploit it to your fullest advantage.

My mentor called these grabbers "transformation mechanisms." It's the idea that you can take someone from point A to point B, and between the two is a twist or an "aha" moment that brings it all together. The twist is when the connection is made, and the moment is fully realized.

One man famous for architecting these aha moments is the "Mad Scientist of Training," Sivasailam Thiagarajan, better known as Thiagi. He's collected and curated hundreds of what he refers to as "jolts"—interactive games and demonstrations that can be used by trainers.[1] In our Trade Show Exhibitor Training, I use one of his jolts to help company representatives remember that their job is to enhance the booth visitor's experience.

In the training, I ask everyone to hold one arm straight out in front of them, then bend it 90 degrees at the elbow and point their index finger up toward the ceiling. Next, I instruct them to draw a clockwise circle with the pointing finger. Once everyone has their clockwise circles going, I tell them to close their eyes and draw their elbows down and in, close to their sides, but keeping their forearms and index fingers still vertical and pointing at the ceiling. With their eyes still closed and fingers still drawing circles, I ask them in which direction their fingers are circling, to which they respond, "clockwise." At this point I instruct them to open their eyes and look at their index fingers. Much to their surprise, they are going around in a counter-clockwise direction.

I love that moment. The looks on their faces say it all—they're confused and searching for an explanation of what they've just experienced. It's usually only a matter of seconds before someone says, "It's because we're looking at it from the other side." The rest of the group will usually smile with acknowledgment and nod in agreement.

Then I ask, "How does this relate to what we're trying to do in the booth at a trade show?" and someone will voice a theory along the lines of, "We need to remember how our guests perceive the exhibit and the booth staff." Of course, I could have just said this at the outset, but because of the interactive experience these company reps just had, the lesson has a greater impact and creates

---

[1] S. Thiagarajan and T. Tagliati, *Jolts! Activities to wake up and engage your participants* (2011).

a lasting impression, resulting in better "boothmanship" at future trade shows.

One of the most common "grabbers" used in speaking is telling a story to teach a lesson while engaging the mind of the listener. The stories don't need to have any initial relevance to the main topic.

A large technology company had reached out to our company to help their presenters develop a more engaging style. Most of their content was very dry, and they were looking for ways to spice things up.

For the coaching session with the sales team, one of the team members was charged with presenting a two-minute presentation for us to review and critique. He started his presentation by sharing that he lives near the mountains. On days when it snows, he sometimes faces a tough decision about whether to do his work that day (from his home office) or to hit the slopes. He then weighed the pros and cons of "playing hooky" from work.

As I listened, I appreciated the departure from the typical technical content and enjoyed getting to know the presenter on a more personal level. As the coach, I was thinking, "I like this. Now pivot to the product and tie it in with your presentation objective." But instead, he ended his presentation. The presentation homework he had prepared focused solely on the tension he felt between his work and the prospect of skiing whenever the slopes were covered with fresh powder.

I quickly surveyed the other participants and asked, "How many of you were waiting for the twist—a tie-in to the technology aspect?" All hands went up.

He had started strong. We were with him—hanging onto his every word, completely on board with his presentation. But we were also curious about how the story would relate back to the company's products. Our neural networks were lit up, looking for the connection. Unfortunately, in this instance, there was no connection to be made, but everyone who was witness to this anti-climactic story received an important lesson: a story can grab the audience's attention and be used to great advantage, but there must be a pay-off in the end.

Hook, grabber, jolt, or transformation mechanism—it matters not what you call it, you just need something to spark engagement.

Why do these work on us?

In an earlier chapter, we discussed the significance of using stories to stimulate the right side of the brain. Props and magic tricks work in a very similar way. When a prop is introduced that seems out of context with the expected content, we are either confused or intrigued by how this prop could be relevant to the presentation. Like a story, it opens a loop that demands closure. Our mind will pay attention, looking for the connection that it craves. This is what was missing from the work versus skiing example from above.

Beyond the convenience of their size, science tells us that there's an additional advantage to using handheld props. Dr. Todd C. Handy, a neuroscientist from Dartmouth University, found that viewing graspable objects stimulated the brain more than objects that cannot be held.[2] In his experiment, Handy connected university students to an electroencephalogram (EEG) machine and compared brain activity when the students looked at pictures of objects such as screwdrivers and coffee mugs versus when they viewed pictures of less graspable objects such as sailboats and cars. He found that when given the choice, the students' attention naturally gravitated to graspable objects.

So, it appears that using a prop that's grabbable as a grabber is the best kind for grabbing attention.

Studies on mirror neurons also suggest that the brain is stimulated just by observing the act of an object being grasped. The original team in Parma, Italy, who discovered mirror neurons, found that

[2] T. Handy, S. Grafton, N. Shroff, S. Ketay, and M. Gazzaniga, "Graspable object grab attention when the potential for action is recognized" in *Nature Neuroscience*, 6, 42–47 (2003). doi: 10.1038/nn1031.

monkeys' mirror neurons showed greater stimulation when an object was used in a familiar motor-neuron action. For example, eating grapes and picking up familiar objects created more neuron activity than operating pliers, as pliers were not only an unfamiliar object to the monkeys, so was their use.

What this means is that when we use a familiar object in front of our audiences, they tend to relate to it because of their knowledge of that object and their experience in handling such an object. A good example of utilizing this scientific fact was on January 15, 2008, when Steve Jobs was on stage at MacWorld launching a new product. He had a common manila envelope beside him on the lectern. He picked it up and pulled out the ultra-thin Mac Book Air. This was a beautiful demonstration of the device's thin form and a dramatic way to reveal the new product.

Another memorable Steve Jobs demonstration was when he revealed the first iPod. After showing slides detailing the look of the iPod, he said, "You can have 1000 songs in your pocket." He then pulled an iPod from his pocket and the crowd went nuts!

When you use a grabber and your audience discovers the twist and sees the connection, that novel moment creates a dopamine spike. The surprise element creates an unexpected reward. These spikes of dopamine become mental sticky notes in our brains. The peaks are remembered as high points and anchor the memory of what happened. This means that our grabbers not only grab attention, but they make your message that much more memorable.

The best way to capture attention and show proof of the value proposition of a product is to present a compelling and highly contrastable demonstration. Some of the best examples of these types of demonstrations can be found in infomercials—paid television or video segments that try to sell a product in a short window of time.

An infomercial demo that shows this well is one for Flex Seal, the rubber spray that can be used for waterproofing and sealing.

The demonstration involves cutting a door-sized hole in a boat and affixing a screen door to the bottom of the hull. Then all the edges of the screen and the entire screen itself are sealed with Flex Seal. Not only does the boat float while someone is in it, it doesn't even leak. TV magic or not, it's an impressive demonstration of the product's effectiveness.

Some products or services can't be easily demonstrated, either because the company sells an intangible product or service, or the actual product is too unwieldy to allow for easy demonstration. This is where creating metaphors becomes so powerful.

When representing companies at trade shows, I have used the medium of magic to create visual metaphors that represent the value my clients bring to the market. Whether transforming one-dollar bills to hundreds as I relate the return on investment that a tech solution offers or discussing the risks of sticking with your current backup solution by playing a game of Russian roulette with staple guns, the prop is not just a prop. It's a representation of a problem, a solution, an end-user, or whatever best serves the narrative in question. Being creative and open-minded are key to creating your own transformation mechanisms.

It's only through trial and error that you find the gimmicks that can help you win people over and get your ideas across. It's only through daring to engage and taking the necessary risks to create a special moment that you discover what works and what doesn't.

Let's take a look at the boxes you need to check when creating your hook. They both start with I—they are *Insight* and *Interrupt*.

Insightful

Your hook must create some sort of *insight* for the recipient or it will fall flat and be a waste of time. Insight is a combination of **connection**, **punch**, and **ownership**. These three elements work together to ensure that people get it.

Connection

Connection is created by clearly drawing a parallel between your transformation mechanism and the point you're trying to make. If the connection is murky or too much of a stretch, people won't make the mental leap and your efforts will go over like a lead balloon. Be very specific and particular about the metaphors and analogies you choose.

One of my clients had a data replication product that could restore lost or deleted data to any point within the previous 21 days. The analogy they liked to use was that of a PVR, a personal video recorder common at the time that allowed the user to pause and rewind live TV but for your data instead. This relatable concept was a perfect analogy to communicate the benefit of the product.

Making connections between ideas and objects is easier than one might think. I often use a brainstorming technique with training groups to illustrate that parallels are easier to find than one might expect. It's called "What does X have to do with Y?" To try this exercise, think of two random objects and consider the ways in which they are similar or could relate to one another. Take one of the objects and ask yourself: What could this object be an example of? When you start with this question, you tend to pull out the qualities of those objects.

Consider the example of two objects, a coat hanger and Play-Doh. At first glance, you might say that one is a device that brings order to your closet and the other is a children's toy. Then ask yourself, "How are these two objects similar? What do they have in common?" Both can be manipulated into different shapes. The coat hanger is an object that was manipulated into the shape of a triangle with its remaining tail shaped into a triangle. Just as the Play-Doh can be manipulated into a shape. More importantly, the coat hanger can be manipulated a further time. With use of a tool such as a pliers, the hanger can be manipulated into a long stick that can be used to roast marshmallows or hot dogs over a campfire. Not only are both Play-Doh and the hanger malleable, but they can also be manipulated over and over again.

I challenge you to try this exercise. To take it to the next level, instead of two objects, pick an object and pair it with a concept or a point you're trying to make. See if you can find a common thread.

In my arsenal of props and metaphors, I have a trick that uses three different lengths of rope. Through the years and over the course of countless trade shows, I've used these ropes to represent all kinds of products and services for my various clients. "Not all companies in this category measure up: some come up short when it comes to…"

Punch

No matter what transformation mechanism you decide to use, it must have punch. That means it has to have a significant impact delivered in as short a time as possible. We've all had a friend who tells stories or jokes with an epically long set-up, only to end with a disappointing punch line. If the joke isn't very funny, it's preferable to keep the set-up short. Or even better, make the joke funnier and the set-up shorter. Now you've got a punchy joke.

$$\text{Punch} = \frac{\text{Impact}}{\text{Time}}$$

The impact of your hook can be improved by raising the stakes. The Flex Seal infomercial could have demonstrated sealing anything at all to keep water out, but without the high stakes it wouldn't have had the same impact. What did they do? They made a boat with a screen door bottom that should have sunk—only it didn't. Putting a passenger in the boat raised the stakes further, increasing the impact even more.

Ownership

The way in which your audience comes to understand a connection is important. When someone discovers a connection for themselves it becomes more powerful because there's greater ownership of the learning. Hitting someone over the head with a lesson isn't as valuable as letting that person learn it for themselves. This is known as *Inductive Learning*. Thinking back to the finger/ceiling/clockwise example, if I had simply said at the outset, "You should look at your booth through the attendee's eyes," it would have gone in one ear and out the other. Allowing an aha moment to happen in someone's mind cements the learning and gives the win to the learner, not the teacher.

Interrupt

Your grabber must do exactly that—grab attention. To be noticed, the grabber must interrupt the pattern that's running in a person's head. It must disrupt the script of what they think will happen.

One of the grabbers I used when doing walkaround magic was exactly that—interruptive.

Let me set the scene: the venue is an upscale ballroom at a hotel or a private club, the crowd is well dressed and well established, and the event is a cocktail reception. I've been hired to entertain the mingling crowd using close-up magic.

My approach was equal parts cheeky and ballsy. I'd walk up to a group and say, "Sorry to interrupt your conversation. Remember your topic and I'll remind you of it when we're through. I'm doing magic here tonight to entertain the guests. Are you guys down to see something amazing?" I would say this with a big smile on my face and all the confidence I could muster. At first, there were looks of surprise, but when they realized I was an entertainer looking to share some fun, they came around.

By saying something different and slightly quirky, I grabbed their attention. How would you get started? How could you get noticed and introduce yourself so you can deliver on what you were hired to do? How can your grabber be a departure from the ordinary?

Create a portfolio

When selecting magic effects for my trade show presentations, I look for material that is message-friendly—something that signifies a change and can be representative of a company or solution. I find that most corporate marketing messages fall into one of three groups.

1. Money—A product or service that will either save you money, or make you money.

2. Time—A product or service that will save you time, and time is money—which is point #1.

3. Peace of mind—A product that will provide an intangible benefit, a feeling of being taken care of, of knowing that your future will be secure because of the product or solution.

I earlier suggested to create a list of your stories and how they relate to different topics or talking points. Create a similar list for your transformation mechanisms. If you ever find a demonstration that ties into the above benefits of money, time, or peace of mind, make a note of it so you can repurpose that content in the future.

Hopefully by now you realize how interesting you can make your content by adding props, stories, demonstrations, and metaphors to better illustrate your point. There really is no end to the various angles you can come up with. The more original you make it, the more memorable you'll be. Be creative and be remembered.

Chapter 13
Creating contrast

When I was a kid, I was an avid watcher of the television show *Sesame Street*. The fact that we only had three channels to choose from may have been partly to blame—*Sesame Street* was one of the few children's shows on the air. One of the recurring segments on the show involved a scene showing four objects with an accompanying song lyric, "One of these things is not like the other." The viewers were then encouraged to spot the one object that had nothing in common with the other three. I remember yelling the answer at those *Sesame Street* characters, wondering why they couldn't hear me.

We are taught at an early age to notice contrast and categorize what we see. It's important to our survival! Our brains are good at noticing change—but not so great at noticing things that remain the same. Our brains tell us that if we are safe and alive right now in this moment—and nothing changes—chances are we will be safe and alive in a short while from now as well. But if something in our circumstances change—a drastic shift in temperature, a sudden feeling of pain, or a bear starting to run towards us—our focus shifts. We must be aware of the changes to ensure our continued survival.

So, standing out and being different are imperative for focus and holding attention. But it's not just about being different as a person. As we described in Chapter 6, we also need to bring contrast to everything we do and say to create engagement.

All the same is lame

Sameness fades to the background of our awareness. As a magician, I know this to be true. In magic, particularly with sleight of hand, a magician is constantly striving to hide certain moves so that the secret behind the trick is not detected, or even suspected. One of the ploys magicians use is to lull spectators into a sense of complacency through using sameness. Let me frame out an example.

A magician is going to make a coin "vanish." The coin will be "tossed" into an open hand, but, in reality, the coin never leaves the tossing hand. To set the audience up, the coin is first *actually* tossed back and forth at least three times to dull the audience's senses to this movement. The last time it's "tossed," it isn't tossed— it's retained in the tossing hand. But as for the people watching, they *expected* the coin to be tossed and so they assume it was.

While magicians are always hiding their work, we want to be highlighting ours. We can do this by looking at what we're saying and how we are saying it and adjusting the qualities of the experience. Everything from how our voice sounds to the kind of content we are presenting and how it's delivered can be adjusted and tweaked to create greater contrast.

My mentor Joel Bauer was the one that first taught me about performing at trade shows and creating engaging presentations. If you've ever seen him perform, you'll never forget the experience. His presentations are some of the most compelling I have ever seen. Whether you liked his approach or not, the results were undeniable; he could hold people spellbound for days at a time. They could not take their eyes off him.

I was fortunate to train with him in Los Angeles on two separate occasions. The first time I saw him, I didn't know what to expect. He came into the ballroom and instantly owned it. He was ultra-confident and immediately launched into stories about his upbringing—how he had spinal meningitis as a toddler, how he didn't speak until he was five years old. Before we knew it, we were being let in on a conference call he held with one of his clients. He held the phone to his microphone so everyone could hear what the client had to say. We moved from one thing to another each story or demonstration designed to frame the ideas he was teaching.

At one point, he teased the unique design of his business card by flashing it briefly to the audience. "I can sell my business cards for $100–$500 each."

That claim was so outlandish I thought, *Yeah right. This I've got to see!*

"For those of you who know my business card, is it effective? Is it worth the money?" he asked the group of 30 trainees.

Some of the attendees more familiar with the speaker nodded in agreement. As for the rest of us, we were confused. How was he going to sell a piece of card stock that cost a few cents for a hundred dollars?

"My business card is no ordinary business card. It doesn't fit in a rolodex because it doesn't belong in a rolodex." Joel brandished his business card; it was about three inches square. He opened the tri-folded card and from the center panel, a pop-up cut-out of Joel himself emerged. "The power of my business card is not about what it is, but what it can do for you. Do you know how much business this card has generated for me? Millions! The first person who comes up the aisle with a $100 bill can have this card."

A few people stirred in their seats and I heard the rustling of bags and the opening of wallets. I sat still. I had no idea where this was going—but I was curious to find out.

Two attendees hurriedly made their way to the front of the room, displaying their banknotes as they approached.

"Could I possibly sell you a piece of worthless paper for $100? Yes, I can. But would that be fair? No, it wouldn't. I'm going to give you more value than that. For the same price, I'll let you use the very same design, the sales copy, and even give you the name of the printer who does them for me. How many of you now in the audience are suddenly thinking the $100 seems like a good deal?"

Right then and there, he sold his business card (and the concept behind it) to two people for $100 each. I was in awe, not only because he was taking money from his audience, but because he had just shown us how to create value from something that was almost worthless. Eventually, of course, he got into the core content of the training and gave us the details and the application of what he was teaching. But anytime he felt the mood shift in the room—when he realized that the audience needed a recharge—he'd shift gears again and tell another story or do another demonstration (one of them involved a bear trap).

Joel would also shift in and out of performance, showing us what the audience would experience and then giving us the peek behind the curtain when he'd come out of performance mode.

The constant flux in content delivery and the shifting of energy and focus made for a roller coaster of a day. Not once did I ever feel that the training was getting long or old. Contrast that (pun intended) with some of the trainings you've attended. Maybe an online session that seemed to go on for days when it was only an hour in length! Or a university class with a dull professor? I always thought it was ironic that a university professor with a doctorate in education could be a horrible teacher. Which goes to show that there is no correlation between education and engagement. Your knowledge is negated if you don't engage.

The power of contrast

The more contrast we create, the more interest we generate. Contrast gets noticed. The number of ways you can change things up boggles the mind. For instance, you can shift the volume and tone of your voice to the kind you would use to tell a secret. Immediately everyone in the room will lean in just a little bit, and you can deliver your hidden gem of an idea to a room full of eager people with bated breath.

These differences that create attention are all around us. Automobile design and marketing often use the Law of Thirds. When they design a new car look, the Law of Thirds suggests that one-third of people will love the car, one-third will hate the car, and the remaining third won't care one way or the other. The perfect example is the Chevrolet Aztec. It had a high backend, which made it very noticeable—ugly, some might say. It also came with a camping tent attachment which could transform the trunk into a sleeping area. Some call it one of the ugliest cars ever built, but it did have its fans, and those fans loved it. Love it or hate it, it got noticed by two-thirds of the people. If you try to make a car (or a presentation) that is unobjectionable, it will be so bland that most people won't take notice.

You must be confident enough in the choices you make that you don't mind the fact that not everyone loves you. Creating contrast and being different means that you and your style may not always fit in.

Let's take a closer look at how you can use contrast to your advantage. In what ways can you shift gears to keep people on their toes?

Changing your body, voice, and space

How often have you ever given a second thought to how you sound? Most of the time, people just open their mouths and say what comes to mind. But without variation in the cadence and style of delivery, your voice will soon be tuned out by your audience. The sound of your voice, the way you speak, can be broken down into six elements—pace, pitch, tonality, intonation, modulation, and volume—and all can be altered and tweaked to create different ways of delivering your information.

How you look can be altered. Your facial expressions and your macro body language can all be varied to create different feelings and thoughts in the audience. Nobody wants to watch a speaker or salesperson who is stone-faced and delivers their pitch or speech standing still.

The space you take up can be used more fully. Whether you're on a real stage, in a boardroom, or on a Zoom call, the visible area around you can be utilized. On stage, it's important to fill up the stage. Use different areas of the stage for different parts of your presentation. In a Zoom call, you can move closer or further away from the camera which creates a zoom-in or zoom-out effect. Both can be used to create contrast in your content.

Using visual aids in new ways

Consider the visuals aids you are using. PowerPoint? Keynote slides? If you use slides in your presentation, you have all kinds of imagery at your fingertips.

Most people recommend having a certain "look" to your slides—branded, with a typical color scheme. But new research suggests that using provocative images to disrupt the pattern established by your standard slides creates a peak state that reinvigorates engagement and makes the content following the high stimulation slide more memorable. What this means is that by strategically placing your pattern-interrupting slides just before the most important parts of your content, attention and retention will be higher.

If you can show slides, you can play videos! As a school student, I remember seeing the cart with the film projector (no videos back then) roll into class, and feeling excited about getting to watch a movie for a change. Even if it was an educational film meant to teach us something, it was a welcome change from a typical school day.

Where the video is located can add depth to your ability to contrast. Jason Reid, a fellow speaker, suggested showing a video in which the speaker is outside in nature. He believes that this change of setting is like a mini mental vacation for viewers. I didn't believe it until I saw it for myself. I felt as if I had physically gone outside for a break. To refresh your audience and renew their attention, film a video outdoors in which you make a salient point that ties into your presentation and just watch the effect it has.

Content variation and props

The style of your content can also be altered for contrast. Are you going to teach the content with a story, a lecture, a game show/quiz format, via panel discussion, group work—all of the above? There are more channels to tap into than you might realize and each shift creates more engagement.

Can you use a prop to help you tell the story? Using an everyday object with qualities that act as a metaphor for your message is both memorable and a great way of changing things up. My professional speaker friend Stephanie Staples once used my office studio for a presentation and brought along cookies—not to eat but as a prop. She used the cookies as a metaphor for treating ourselves or taking moments for self-care, emphasizing that we all need a "cookie" once in a while.

A prop is an interesting tool because the presence of the object creates a story gap and makes people want to know: *What does this object have to do with anything you are going to say?* When you make your allusion clear and spell out how it relates to your topic, the audience experiences an "aha" moment in which they put the pieces together and everything makes sense. Having to make this mental leap gives the recipient ownership of the learning while the novelty factor of the prop makes the interaction more memorable.

Using props is a great way of contrasting what you do with what might be expected.

If you are presenting virtually, whether over Zoom or a similar platform, you can have all kinds of fun changing camera angles to change your audience's perspective. Video overlays or special lighting as noted in an earlier chapter are only two of many options at your disposal. The elements of any interaction have qualities that can be altered to create something new and exciting to win the attention of your prospect or audience member.

Creating more contrast—in summary

Divide the parts of your presentation into different categories according to the delivery method or pace dynamics. Are you using direct lecture, slides on a big screen, whiteboarding some ideas, asking questions of the audience, telling a joke, and so on? If you find that your main activity is primarily only one method, you might need to find ways of changing things up.

In the same vein, look at your content—does it have long sections that could be broken up with some type of contrast? Could you stand in a different place on stage for each different segment? Could you walk into the audience while presenting?

How can you change what your audience sees? Can you use more facial expressions and body language while telling your story? Can you use an image or slide to get your point across? Would a video clip be more effective?

What are the sounds your audience hears? How can you create contrast? Can you add music? Or create more vocal variety?

What do you want your audience to feel? Is this a purely intellectual interaction, or would it be more interesting if they were more emotionally involved? How could you orchestrate that?

Is what you're doing different enough for people to take notice?

Chapter 14
Creating deep connection

What does the word "rapport" mean to you? Some sources define it as a harmonious relationship in which people communicate ideas and understand each other's feelings well.

I used to think that this kind of connection happened only by chance—that you either clicked with someone or you didn't. As a sales professional, I have read many books on the art of sales and several of them mention rapport and the value of developing rapport early in a meeting or a relationship. According to these books, developing rapport meant finding common ground, like sharing a hobby, a mutual acquaintance, or a similar devotion to a particular sports team. But in practice, this "rapport building" looked more like a fishing expedition as the salesperson queries the prospect to find commonalities—or worse, fakes an interest in the prospect's interests.

It wasn't until I developed an interest in NLP that I started to understand that there's a process or structure to creating rapport. Knowing this process has made it became possible for me to deepen connections with anyone, no matter what their hobbies or background.

NLP is a field of psychology founded by Richard Bandler and John Grinder in the early 1970s. It grew from their observation and modeling of three therapists who were producing amazing results with their patients. The therapists were Virginia Satir, Fritz Perls, and Milton Erickson. Virginia Satir was an American psychotherapist who was recognized for her approach to family therapy. Her pioneering work in the field of family reconstruction therapy honored her with the title "Mother of Family Therapy." Fritz Perl was a German-born psychiatrist, psychoanalyst, and psychotherapist who coined the term "Gestalt therapy" to identify the form of psychotherapy that he developed in the 1940s and 1950s. Erickson was known as the first hypnotherapist and was called the "Wizard of the Dessert" because of his magic-like ability to help people with their problems.

Bandler and Grinder would watch Erickson at work, observing him for hours at a time and noting his every move. Before long they recognized patterns and were able to codify exactly what was involved in Erickson's approach (both what he said and what he did). Erickson was quoted as saying that, "With rapport, anything is possible; without it, nothing is." His hypnotic work with his patients' unconscious mind was possible only because of the deep rapport he could establish.

Equipped with the steps needed to generate rapport, Bandler and Grinder set out to teach these steps to their students, combining their findings with other NLP patterns.

To get a sense of what rapport looks like from afar, start watching people—really watching. Couples dining in restaurants are a great subject for gauging rapport. Somehow you just know which couples are on a first date, which ones are madly in love, which ones have been together for a long time, and which ones aren't exactly "clicking." Their body language tells the story. Couples that are deeply connected are in sync with one another. The angle in which they sit is similar, their head tilts and arm positions seem to be duplicated. In fact, it's as if they are mirroring each other.

Mirroring and matching

Mirroring and matching is the phrase that the NLP founders used to describe the physical aspect of creating rapport. This act occurs quite naturally and unconsciously all the time. In fact, it's pretty fascinating to catch yourself in rapport with someone you're talking to. The first few times you notice it happening, it can be quite surprising.

Mirroring is what you see in the figure above: two people facing each other, one person's right arm up and the other person's left arm up, creating a mirror image.

Matching, on the other hand, is mimicking your counterpart's action but with the same hand/arm/foot, and so on. If their right leg is crossed over their left, you cross your right over left.

This process of taking on similar body positions bonds you to the other person; the more we are alike, the more we like. This phenomenon of rapport built on matching and mirroring is called the "chameleon effect."

In 1999, two professors of psychology at New York University conducted experiments that studied this phenomenon. They wanted to know if this unconscious mimicry would increase their likeability and whether people who are more agreeable would display the chameleon effect more often.

What Chartrand and Bargh discovered was that unconscious mimicking created a higher likability, and that those people who are readily agreeable tended to mimic even more. Chartrand noted that "Those who pay more attention, mimic more", resulting in higher likability and more friends.[1]

Although NLP first codified this phenomenon in the 1970s, it wasn't until the mid-1990s that scientists could actually prove it exists and understand why. In Parma, Italy, a group of researchers led by Giancomo Rizzolatti experimented with macaques (monkeys).[2] They attached implants to the monkeys' brains in order to measure neural activity. They were interested in finding out which neurons would fire when the monkeys performed specific actions such as grabbing a grape and eating it. What they discovered—by accident—was that the neurons that fired in the monkey when it grabbed a grape and ate it, also fired if the monkey watched a researcher (on their lunch) take a grape and eat it.

Rizzolatti and his team also found that individual neurons would only respond to specific actions. One neuron might fire for holding the grape (either the monkey or the researcher holding the grape) while another neuron would fire when the grape was eaten (by monkey or experimenter). This breakthrough in research has led to discoveries in empathy, social dynamics, and learning. As Rizzolatti's research partner, Vittorio Gallese, says, "It seems we're wired to see other people as similar to us, rather than different. As humans, we identify the person we're facing as someone like ourselves."

---

[1] T. L. Chartrand and J. A. Bargh, "The chameleon effect: The perception–behavior link and social interaction" in *Journal of Personality and Social Psychology*, 76 (6), 893–910 (1999). doi: 10.1037/0022-3514.76.6.893.

[2] G. Rizzolatti and L. Craighero, "The mirror-neuron system" in *Annual Review of Neuroscience*, 27, 169–192 (2004). doi: 10.1146/annurev.neuro.27.070203.144230. PMID: 15217330.

In other words, we're wired to get along with others. Mirror neurons help us understand what others are feeling—they are the very roots of empathy.

What does this mean to us in terms of engagement? To connect with someone on a deeper level, you need to develop rapport. Developing rapport makes people instantly like you and trust you. When this is possible, communication becomes almost effortless… and timeless.

Have you ever been in such deep and fascinating conversation that you felt as if you were in a time warp? I remember having a conversation with a fellow performer during a five-hour drive. The drive felt like only 20 minutes and yet my voice was getting hoarse from the length of the conversation we had. When you're in rapport, you feel as you fully understand the other person and you are in the "flow." Psychologist Robert Dilts calls this flow "a loop of mutual influence."

If you could deepen your connection to the people you interact with, what could that mean for your selling, your relationships, or your next negotiation at the bargaining table?

One of the exercises I use when teaching rapport at an in-person training event begins with dividing participants into groups of two. Each pair of people must come up with a topic on which they can debate and take opposite sides. There are parameters, such as prohibiting topics involving religion or politics. People often end up debating the superiority of one sports team or athlete over another. Then they are directed to have the same debate twice—the first time without any rapport; that is, no mirroring or matching.

The second time, they are told to mirror and match in order to foster rapport. The differences between the first and second debate are startling. The second debate, in which participants are seeking rapport through the use of mirroring and matching, has noticeably less conflict and more cooperation. I've even overheard one participant say: "I didn't want to see their side of things, but I couldn't help it."

It's no wonder these techniques are used and taught by negotiation experts and even hostage negotiators.

How to mirror and match

First, look at the angle of your counterpart's spine. Are they leaning forward or reclined back in their chair? Matching the spinal angle of the other person is particularly important. If you don't believe it, try having a conversation with someone while you're both seated and deliberately mismatch their posture. It doesn't feel right—in fact, it almost feels rude.

Next, observe their extremities. They may have their legs or arms crossed—a behavior that's easily matched. When you first start becoming aware of rapport it's very common to see people speaking to each other with arms crossed. Once you start to look for it, it's everywhere.

A note on timing

Mirroring and matching is not mimicry. You are not trying to mirror a person's movements in real time. Delaying your movements by up to 20 seconds is enough "time misdirection" to throw them off the scent. If the person you're conversing with detects that you're mirroring them, you're matching too soon.

Macro versus micro

Some people talk with their hands frequently and gesture expressively. Trying to match this type of body language may feel out of place to you if you're not prone to being as expressive. If this is the case, you may want to try using micro movements to match their macro movements. For example, if someone moves their whole arm to point in a certain direction, you might reciprocate by just pointing with your hand or your fingers. Playing down the gesture in size and intensity can make it more natural in the moment.

Crossover matching

There are other physical ways in which we can sync up. Some people may tap their foot or rock gently as a means of burning nervous energy. You can match that tapping in subtle ways, further connecting the two of you. Whether you tap a finger silently on your leg or tap your foot to the nodding of their head, there are a multitude of ways to synchronize your movements and deepen connection.

In addition to your body language, how you speak can also build rapport. Note the pace, tone, and cadence of the other person's speech patterns. By subtly matching the way they speak, you can increase your shared bond. Again, it's important not to mimic. We are not doing an impersonation of them. If they have a soft, airy voice, slightly soften yours. If they speak slower than you do, slow down to match.

This is much like shaking someone's hand. Our perception of the handshakes of others is in comparison to the one we are offering. Some people shake too hard and come off as aggressive or over the top; some have a limp handshake, which can seem passive and submissive. The ones who shake just right are the ones that are matching our own pressure and style of shake.

In addition to vocal rapport, you can build rapport with your words. If the person you are speaking with uses particular vocabulary, you can use those same words and they'll feel listened to and understood.

You may be familiar with the three learning styles, visual, auditory, and kinesthetic (or VAK). While we tend to use a mixture of the three, most of us have one style that we prefer over the others. Our preferences can be detected in our speech patterns. People who are visual tend to use visual predicates.

They'll say things like:

I want to *show* you...

Can you *see* here that...?

That should *clear* things up...

By now you probably get the *picture*.

From auditory people, you'll hear things like:

That *rings* a bell.

Can you *tell* me more about...?

I like the *sound* of that.

What I'm *hearing* is...

That *rings* true.

Kinesthetic speakers speak in terms of feelings. You'll hear them say:

That's a real *solid* choice.

I *feel* that...

That *resonates* with me.

Do you *feel* me?

With careful practice, you'll be able to pick up on each person's preferred modality. By using the same sensory speech patterns when you speak with them, they will feel as if you understand them—you're both speaking the same language.

In the early days of NLP, when Bandler and Grinder were still experimenting, they invited a group of people to a gathering.

Upon entry, each individual received a nametag with one of three differently colored stickers on it. The attendees were instructed to mingle with one another but to speak only with people whose nametags had a sticker that was a different color from their own.

At this point in the evening, nothing out of the ordinary could be observed. But then Bandler and Grinder stopped everyone and announced that they should speak only to the people with the same color nametag. Instantly, the noise level in the room rose as a result of all the animated discussions going on. Prior to the gathering, Bandler and Grinder had determined which representational system was preferred by each attendee—V, A, or K—and had assigned a color to each of these three groups.

The experiment reinforced the concept that when you're with "your" people, you feel the most comfortable and hit it off most naturally.

Next-level rapport

By now you can probably see that observational skills are a must for this kind of rapport development. If you are ready to take your rapport skills to the next level, try this, watch a person's shoulders when they breathe and try to sync your breathing to theirs.

Group rapport

We have explored one-to-one situations, but how can we build rapport with a group of people? They all have different VAK preferences, so how can you mirror and match multiple people at once?

Bonding a group of people to you can be accomplished in various ways. One is through **forced rapport**. This means asking them/ telling them to do as you do.

Let's pretend for a moment that all the readers of this book are in an audience and I'm on stage, teaching this content. As I raise my own hand in the air, I would say something like, "Raise your hand right now if you are here to learn how to engage at higher level." Most likely, every hand in the room would go up in the air.

Another way to create group rapport is through group action. Street performers often use a rhythmic clap to unite their audiences. As they're about to attempt some trick or feat of skill, they'll get the audience to clap slowly in unison, gradually speeding up the rhythm. As the individuals clap along with the rest of the audience and the performer, they meld into one entity of energy. This group rapport increases everyone's enjoyment of the show as each individual feeds off the energy of their fellow audience members.

Stealing rapport

Stealing rapport is a little trick that can be used if you're following a well-received speaker on stage or if there's a very likable emcee hosting an event.

To steal rapport, when it's your turn to take the stage, stand exactly where the previous person was standing. Start your presentation by speaking in a similar tone and pace as that presenter. Gradually you can return to your usual style of delivery, but by that time you should have the audience on-side and willing to follow you.

The reverse holds true as well. If the person preceding you is not well-liked by the audience, don't stand where they were standing, and try to adopt a different tone and pace in your speaking. The audience will welcome the change of pace and will latch on to you as a breath of fresh air.

Pacing and leading

Pacing people's actions and language through mirroring and matching results in a deeper connection and more effective communication. But what if just pacing them where they are at is not what you want or need?

Once I was performing magic at an association's Annual General Meeting. The president of the association was finishing up his speech and was about to introduce the evening's entertainment—me—when he mentioned the passing of a long-time member and past president. "Let's all bow our heads in a moment of silence to remember Jim. Twenty seconds later, he continued, "Okay, let's bring out the magician."

Not the note I like to start my show on. Normally, I'd hit the stage fired up and ready to get people excited about the show they're about to experience. But doing that in this instance would have been rude and unwise. Instead, I paced the energy of the room. I spoke more slowly and solemnly and asked the audience if it would be alright to show them something kind of interesting. The audience collectively nodded their heads, granting permission. After that I slowly started increasing the pace of my speech up to my normal rate.

The same is true in your one-on-one interactions. Through mirroring and matching, you can start to lead a person once it's clear that you've gained rapport. Maybe the person you're talking with is sitting back, arms crossed—possibly signaling boredom or disinterest. Once you think that rapport has been established, you can test by making the first move. Sit forward or uncross your arms, or both. Watch and see what happens next—chances are they will follow.

Chapter 15
This time it's personal

Hey, you! Yeah you—the person reading this book! I'm talking to you! What I'm about to share with you in this chapter can dramatically change the results you get in life and the way people interact with you on a daily basis. Have I got your attention?

What if the above paragraph, instead of using the word "you," actually used your name? It would freak you out a bit, right? Imagine if the book was personalized to that extent for each reader; it would be hard to put down and difficult to ignore.

Author Robert C. Lee said, "The sweetest sound to anyone's ears is the sound of his own name."[1] Dale Carnegie, of *Win Friends and Influence People* fame, said something similar: "A person's **name** is to that person, the **sweetest**, most important **sound** in any language."[2]

Our names are so personal to us that we can't help but listen, look, and take notice when we hear them. It's the analog equivalent of a smartphone notification. It tells us that someone wants to

---

[1] R. C. Lee, *The Sweetest Sound to Anyone's Ears Is the Sound of His Own Name* (n.d.).

[2] D. Carnegie, *How to Win Friends and Influence People* (1936).

tell us something or ask us something. Whatever is happening, it most definitely is concerning us. The grabbing of our immediate attention goes beyond just our names—we're interested in anything that has to do with us.

However, so many things in life have nothing to do with us. The fire truck that comes roaring down the street is in a hurry, but we're not concerned if we know it's not a fire at our house; same with the junk emails that aren't remotely related to your life and situation. We're bombarded with stimulation, and for the brain to make sense of all of it, we must delete, distort, and generalize that information to make it manageable. We filter everything that comes our way so we can deal with the sheer volume of stimuli. That filter is always tuned in to anything that personally involves us. It's intended to be this way as a means of survival.

From an evolutionary standpoint, it's imperative to pay attention to anything that will personally benefit you (food, a mate, money, etc.) and anything that could threaten you (oncoming traffic, a saber-toothed tiger, etc.). Your survival ensures the propagation of your genes.

Subsequently, the more we cater to our audiences and demonstrate that a message is just for them, the more engagement we'll create.

Before I founded my company, I performed magic full time at conferences and corporate events. Before my main after-dinner presentation, I would often be hired to perform close-up magic during the cocktail hour. During that hour, I'd interact with as many as 60–70 different people as I invited them to participate in the interactive portions of my close-up magic. Every time someone helped me with a trick, I would ask their name. Upon hearing the name, I would repeat it back immediately—out loud—which provided that person confirmation of what I heard. Using a person's name as soon as possible, and saying it aloud as I looked at them, helped to anchor their name in my memory.

Sometimes I would use one of the various mnemonic techniques that I've learned over the years to connect the person to the name.

Then, every time I saw that person walking around the venue, I would say their name silently in my head.

The upshot of all of this was that by the time I was ready to begin the after-dinner show, I had memorized roughly 20 names from the audience. During my performance I would focus on choosing those people as volunteers for the show, saying, "It's Jessica, right?" or "Steve, why don't you come up here and help me?" and each person would be tickled that I had remembered them. After working with just a handful of these remembered people, the audience sometimes became convinced that I had memorized the names of every single audience member! I hadn't, of course, but I didn't mind taking credit for it.

This memory game I played for myself added an extra layer of specialness to the performance. It was something that couldn't be faked—it was happening just for that audience, in the moment and with their names! The show didn't feel canned or templated because adding names into the performance completely personalized the experience.

In addition to learning names, I would ask every client to fill out a Custom Comedy Questionnaire about a month before the event in order to better understand the company culture—the background, inside jokes, memorable incidents, and anything that could make the performance more special.

Improv, which we discuss briefly in the "Yes and..." chapter is another good example of customization and personalization. If you've ever seen great improv, you know how amazing it is to watch a story being crafted in real time from suggestions offered by the audience. The improvisers create a story that's never been told before and will never be seen again. Because this story is being created in the here and now, for an audience lucky enough to witness it, there's a real sense of specialness to the content. Individual audience members understand that it's a story being made just for them, even if every member of the audience is having the same thought.

Treating every individual the same, every time, is a sure way to turn off your audience and be forgotten before you were ever really noticed in the first place.

In no context is this more common than in customer service. Whether it's the cashier at a grocery store, a flight attendant, or a server at a restaurant, at one time or another, they slip into the habit of saying the same things over and over to the point that they don't really know what they are saying anymore; you know they say it to everybody, and, in fact, they may even repeat themselves while serving you. Maybe you've had a cashier ask you when you reach the till, "Did you find everything you were looking for?" and then again, they ask just 30 seconds later while bagging your items.

It's like watching a performance so rote that the audience doesn't really need to be there. An old Vegas lounge act comes to mind for me, in which the performer repeats the same jokes, the same dialogue, at the exact same time for every audience, every night. When something feels canned, it negates your individuality. It says that this is good enough for you no matter who you are. It sends the message that you aren't special in a world where everybody wants to feel special.

When I started getting first-class upgrades and flight attendants called me "Mr. Boulanger," I was initially a little taken aback. Of course, they have access to a flight manifest that lets them know who's sitting where, and to give that extra bit of a customer service touch, they look up the first-class passengers. When you know their name and they know yours, it creates the foundation for a deeper connection. When we officially "meet" someone, exchanging names is the first thing we do. How far the relationship may go from there is hard to say, but at least the important first step has been completed.

It comes down to making the interaction special so that it stands out in a person's mind. Uniqueness breaks the script of what they thought would happen. The more you can tailor your presentation to your audience, the more they'll take notice. Even if the customization works for every prospect/customer, the fact that you took the time to customize it in the first place is admirable.

Even before the pandemic, my company had been selling virtually for years—through teleconferencing and video conferencing platforms. To sell our trade show lead generation services, we would meet with the potential clients' marketing teams and walk them through a slide presentation explaining our value proposition. Many of the presentation techniques we developed back then still have an important place in our sales presentations today.

For example, to make the slide deck more engaging for each team, we take the time to customize it to the greatest extent possible; of course, showcasing the potential client's company name on the title slide is a no-brainer.

Next, to build credibility and authority, we share a slide of client logos, showcasing the companies we've worked with over the years. This is both common and expected; but then we do something that isn't. Using the PowerPoint animations, a couple of the logos move around to create an open space. "If we just move these out of the way—there we go—hopefully there's enough room," I'll say, and at that moment their own company logo appears in the midst the other client logos. "Perfect—it fits!" I say, tongue-in-cheek. The maneuver results in a laugh and a smile—at the very least.

"Seriously, can you see yourselves working with our company and becoming one of our clients?" This gag has now evolved into a question that is measuring buying intent.

The typical response is along the lines of, "Possibly, if we can check all the right boxes."

"Excellent, let's figure out what those boxes are then." Now we're getting at the root of what the buying criteria will be.

A few slides later, I share a picture of the company's actual trade show booth, nabbed from the internet. I then illustrate how the presence of a trade show infotainer at the corner of the booth can attract crowds of interested attendees. As I explain this, a small stage appears with a picture of one of our infotainers in action and a large crowd of people approaching the booth. The effect of the animations, illustrating the results that our services can have, helps to create a powerful mental image. The effort taken to tailor the presentation is also appreciated.

Count the "yous" and "yours"

One of the biggest mistakes salespeople make is to lead with their solution or company and make it all about them. This is not just an issue in sales either. When I first met my wife, I was guilty of talking about myself—a lot. As a performer, I was accustomed to having people talk about me, since being a magician is unusual and fascinating for many. I hadn't yet discovered the power of making your content "you-focused."

The next time you write an email, pause before you hit "send." Review what you wrote and count how many times you wrote "you," "yours," "your company," the prospect's company's name or anything else that refers to the recipient. Then compare that to the number of times you wrote "we," "I," "mine," "ours," and anything involving your own company.

If you're truly writing with your audience in mind, it should be about them, not you. The occurrences of "you" and "yours" should outnumber references to yourself and your company. If they don't, go back and rewrite the email until they do. This will be a revealing exercise for many people, as it highlights our tendency to put ourselves first.

The same exercise can be done by looking at a transcript of one of your virtual meetings. Go to Otter.ai and upload a video. This service will transcribe the video, giving you a quick and easy way to review what was said in the meeting, and revealing whether you were focused on the other person or more focused on what you had to offer.

Break the script

If you're in a customer-facing role in your company, strive to make your interactions unique, giving the people you interact with the same feeling that an audience at an improv show would have. Make your "performance" a one-off, giving people the sense that your comments and actions are custom-tailored—not learned from a script that's repeated without variation to every client.

Embrace each person as an individual and craft a response appropriate to the situation instead of just using the words your training manual tells you to say. The more you break the script, the more memorable you'll be. Make them glad they were here for this.

Make the effort

Personalizing and customizing presentations and interactions requires effort, and it is certainly far easier to do the bare minimum, go through the motions, and say what you would usually say. But that doesn't serve you or the other person in any way.

Take the time and prepare. In time, you'll find shortcuts and hacks that will shave time off your preparations. (I've become so fast at creating my initial meeting presentation, I could put it together five minutes before a meeting if I needed to.)

Memorize names

A lot of people say things like "I'm terrible with names!" Some people even say this right as you're meeting them—"I'll probably forget your name right away." Wow. Thanks a lot. We just met and you're already telling me I'm forgettable.

If you're like most people, you're not terrible with names—you've just never learned to use your memory effectively. I find that just priding yourself on being better with names and faces improves your results. Too many people are hard on themselves and as a result, don't even bother trying. Make the effort and become one of the special few who blow people away with their attention to detail. By remembering someone's name you're showing them that they're important, which really cuts to the heart of what we all want as humans—to know that we matter.

Chapter 16
Humor is serious business

I think we can say that most people like to laugh. It not only *feels* good to laugh, laughter does the body good. According to the Mayo Clinic, laughter can relieve tension, reduce pain, stimulate organs, and improve your immune system.[1] So the old saying of laughter being the best medicine has some truth to it.

Creating laughter has other positive effects. Through humor, we're able to instantly create a positive feeling in others. I have several comedian friends and they all exhibit the same drive to create a smile and get a laugh. Not only does it make the recipient feel good, but the positive effect gives the joke teller a rush as well.

We already know that when you apply emotion to any situation, the event becomes more memorable. It's why we remember really funny things that happen to us, sometimes inspiring stories that become legendary in their repeated re-telling for friends and family. The addition of emotion elevates the moment and makes the experience stand out in our minds. Humor is a powerful

---

[1] L. S. Berk and S. A. Tan, "The effect of laughter on health: A systematic review of the literature" in *International Journal of Humor Research*, 22 (4), 415–434 (2009).

tool to help you differentiate yourself and be remembered in the minds of others.

However, humor is often misunderstood. Humor and jokes can be confused for one another. Jokes are the lines and structure—a way of creating humor. Humor is the viewpoint and the attitude that sees the lighter side of things. Jokes are scripted recipes; humor is seeing the funny in the situation.

In this chapter, my goal is not to get you to be like your weird uncle who has a stock line for every occasion. This is not about turning yourself into a class clown. Instead, I want to explain how developing and embracing your sense of humor can be a powerful tool to create engagement.

In the business world in particular, we tend to put our sense of humor in the back seat. We assume that being professional means being serious. That's baloney! The levity created by good-humored managers and team members is what makes many jobs tolerable.

Recently I was training a group of people who were very reluctant to film videos that were required for their jobs. My company was tasked with increasing their comfort level in front of the camera so they could effectively produce the video content that was required of them.

We had already been coaching this group for a number of weeks, which was advantageous because they needed to be comfortable with each other as well as with me. I needed their trust before I could gently coax them out of their comfort zones.

One of the exercises I had them do was to present their one-minute prepared talk but embodying an archetype instead of their normal personas.

Some of the options were:

- The Giant (moves and talks real big)
- The kindergarten teacher (uses high vocal modulation and lots of expression)

▶ The conspiracy theorist (speaks in a paranoid whisper)

▶ The storyteller (spins a yarn for the folks listening)

▶ The seducer (woos the audience in a sultry voice)

Participants were divided into groups of two and instructed to use an archetype as far removed from their true selves as possible—something that would be a real stretch. One of the two partners would present their one-minute presentation while imbuing the chosen archetype with its associated characteristics. Then the other partner was to suggest which part of that archetype they should keep in their repertoire.

This is a fascinating exercise because while people are playing over-the-top, one-dimensional roles—which can be quite funny to watch—in the end there's always a redeeming and valuable element within each of the archetypes. The conspiracy theorist, for example, compels people to lean in and listen more closely (even in virtual meetings); the kindergarten teacher causes even the most stone-faced, monotone speaker to become animated and engaging.

On this particular occasion, after two rounds with this group, a participant named Raissa spoke up. "This exercise allowed me to discover things that are a part of me, but I never really realized it until now," she said. "It feels like I'm bringing out more of my personality. This revealed that I'm not truly being myself in meetings and professional settings."

This was a big "aha" for the entire group, as the feeling was mutual. Many of us have played it safe for so long, we've forgotten how to lighten up. We don't think of looking for the funny that is happening all around us. We don't fully express our true selves in professional situations. Being engaging is about being more of who you really are, which creates interest and texture for those around us. Having a healthy sense of humor is just one way to endear ourselves to those with whom we would like to engage.

Here's the caveat: humor can be subjective. What's funny to me may not be funny to you; what's funny in your culture may not be funny in the next person's culture; what was funny 20 years ago may not be funny today. One reason some people play it safe is that it's just easier not to take the risk. I remember going with friends to see a mentalist (mind reading magician) in Las Vegas. The way he treated the female volunteers in his show disgusted the lot of us. His material and performing style hadn't aged well. Society had evolved but his act hadn't.

To be successful in employing humor, it's integral that you're tuned in to what is acceptable and what isn't; and when in doubt, leave it out.

With this warning in mind you might be thinking, is it worth it? Maybe it's best to keep comments to myself and not risk it?

Based on my performing experience of almost 30 years, I know for a fact that it is worth it. The value of humor and what it can do for you in your personal interactions is huge! There's an old saying in the professional speaking industry that goes: "Do you have to be funny to be a professional speaker?" and the response is: "Only if you want to be paid!"

Just like the act of engaging with someone in the first place, there are risks built in, but the rewards are worth it.

Humor is a powerful tool for instantly connecting with someone and breaking down the barriers that separate you. When people know that you're having fun with them, there's a sense of relief. They're relieved because they no longer have to carefully read the situation. They understand that you're not a threat—you've bridged the divide that was between you by having some fun. This breaking of the ice is really a release of tension. Humor works by building tension and then releasing it. For example, with a joke, the set-up is the tension-creating piece that opens the story loop. The punchline then releases the tension by making a connection or observation that we find to be true.

Adding emotion to your message creates a mental sticky note in a person's mind, but this might be tricky if we didn't have humor in our arsenal. Most salespeople would agree that we don't want to make the people we meet sad, angry, or jealous just to improve the memorability of our message. Making people happy and giving them a laugh is the easiest and most practical way of going about this.

Humor is a powerful tool for building rapport. If you'll recall from Chapter 14 on rapport, the more we are like someone, the more they will tend to like you. Sharing humor puts a smile on both your faces—you may even both end up laughing. These mirrored emotions and responses connect us and bond a group together. Want to build rapport? Share something you can both find funny.

Humor me

What steps can you take to bring more humor into your interactions? Here are some ideas:

Tone is everything

I have a friend named Richard Laible, who is probably the funniest person I know. He's a product of Second City Theater in Chicago and has shared the stage with a number of *Saturday Night Live* alums. One of the things I appreciate about the way Richard interacts is his tone of voice. He has a way of saying things that makes you feel like a punchline is coming at any minute (it usually is). He can say almost anything to anyone and get away with it, mostly because of the way he says it.

Watch a comedian like Jim Gaffigan or Ricky Gervais sometime and listen to how they say their material and feel their rhythm. There's a certain sound quality they possess that just sounds light-hearted and naturally funny. Try experimenting with how you say things—try speaking with a huge smile on your face, for example. How does it change the quality of your voice?

Make sure your sense of humor is shared by everyone and try your best to avoid possibly offensive remarks. If you're going to pick on someone, pick on yourself and make self-deprecating remarks, but don't overdo it. Excessive self-deprecation without a certain degree of genuine confidence behind it can create a feeling of pity from your audience—which quickly pulls the humor and fun from the situation.

Ultimately, cultivating a sense of humor that sees the funny in the moment without picking on anyone is the best way to go.

Calling the moment

"Calling the moment" is a phrase comedian and comedy guru, Judy Carter, uses to describe a situation where someone states the obvious. It could be during an awkward moment, a lack of reaction to a joke, or any mutual experience between two or more people. It harnesses the built-up tension in a situation and releases that tension by stating aloud what everyone is thinking. Calling it out clears the air and acknowledges a reality everyone knows to be true. Generally speaking, this is a safe moment of levity that can be created in all sorts of situations.

You might recall my anecdote from an earlier chapter, in which I was riding a very narrow escalator packed full of people in the Atlanta Convention Center. I said loudly enough for everyone to hear, "Could these escalators be any narrower!" and everybody started to chuckle and riff off that comment. This is an example of calling the moment.

Know thyself and know thy audience

Trusting yourself in the moment is critical. Your gut will tell you when to strike and when to hold back with a quip or comment. You know what you're capable of and you know what you can get away with. With time you'll find your "sweet spot" and hone your comedic point of view. Even so, test yourself from time to time.

Don't let your past rule your future—see if you can stretch a bit here and there and you might surprise yourself.

Knowing your audience is especially important. I vividly remember an occasion when a comedian spoke to our professional speaking association chapter about putting comedy into a presentation. Towards the end of his talk, he made a point about knowing your audience—which was ironic, as 15 minutes earlier he had made an off-color joke that didn't go over well with our group. The chatter following his talk was that he did not practice what he preached. He had unwittingly demonstrated how important knowing your audience is.

Say it with a smile

Ever deal with someone who's hard to read? Not sure if they're kidding or serious? Make sure you are not one of these people. Make it easy for people to guess your intentions—make those intentions abundantly clear, by using the appropriate body language and tone. The easiest way of doing that is to show it in your face. A mischievous grin is all that's required for someone to know where you're coming from. With a smile you say that you mean no harm and you came to play.

Chapter 17
Engaging with your voice

Unless you're a singer, a speaker or an actor, chances are you don't give your voice a second thought. Ever since you were born you've been able to communicate through sound—even if it was simply by crying.

We open our mouths and we just talk. It just happens. It's very similar to breathing in many ways. We've been doing it all our lives and we pretty much have it nailed. Or so we think.

The more you study communication, the more you begin to realize it's more than just the words you say, it's also how you say them. I think of this every time I get off a long flight and a worn-out flight attendant gets on the mic and says in a flat, monotone voice, "Welcome to Orlando, where the time is now 3 pm. *It's been our pleasure to serve you. Thank you for flying Delta."* The last part never feels real—in part because we know it's a script that's repeated day in and day out, but also because of how it's said. If it were truly a pleasure, the flight attendant would say it in way that would cause us to *feel* her message instead of just hearing it.

These incongruous communications happen all the time. Often, it's because there's a script involved, and people just follow what it says instead of voicing each word as if it actually means something to them.

Recently, I was emceeing a virtual sales kick-off for a billion-dollar company. Each of the C-level executives was given time to update the sales force on the previous year's successes and share plans for the coming year. One executive decided to read his PowerPoint notes, presumably so he wouldn't miss anything. This became monotonous very quickly. When we read anything word for word, we tend to come off very flat unless we make the extra effort to make our delivery more engaging.

When we think of words as we say them, our minds are busy putting things together, our voices are accentuating specific words to create meaning and our bodies are working in tandem to further express the idea we're trying to get across. We do this all unconsciously, but when we read, all this goes out the window.

This chapter will provide you with ideas of how to be more engaging by paying special attention to your voice. Actors spend their lives cultivating their skills to create more on-stage or on-screen presence, and working on their voices is a major part of that effort.

From 1995 to 1999, I attended Brandon University. It's a small campus of just 2000 students and located only 30 minutes from my hometown. I was in the Faculty of Science, pursuing my Bachelor of Science degree in physics, but I needed to take some Arts (humanities) courses in order to remain human. With my background in magic, I was understandably drawn to the theater courses. The high school in my tiny hometown didn't have a drama department so this was my first experience "treading the boards."

When I walked into class for the first time, I saw an interesting mix of students, most of whom looked nothing like me. I was a typical jeans and T-shirt kind of guy, surrounded by darkly clad arts students who accessorized with scarves and berets.

I like the arts—don't get me wrong—but it was never my goal to be "artsy." On my first day, a student from the School of Music rhapsodized about how "you must treat your voice as a Stradivarius." I thought to myself: "Give me a break!" That attitude was fine for them, but I had a much more utilitarian approach to acting. I wasn't interested in doing the work; I just wanted to do the scene.

Every class, we did a physical warm-up—a series of stretches and movement exercises to get our blood flowing—and then we would do a vocal warm-up. We warmed up our voices by echoing the noises and phrases that our professor "projected" our way. It always felt kind of silly, but I figured that's just what you do in theater— the price of admission for participating in the rest of class.

After completing university, I paid to participate in a week-long performer's retreat taking place in the foothills of Montreal. It was situated at a picturesque lakeside resort. Every attendee (10 in total) was a magician, a juggler, or some sort of variety artist. We each brought with us a 10-minute act that we were to workshop.

The workshop was conducted by two veteran Broadway actors and directors who brought a theatrical perspective to our performances. Bob Fitch, the founder and principal of this retreat, was passionate about creating world-class performers. His performance philosophy was that it wasn't just one thing that made a performer great but a combination of layers that accumulated over time. There was a force multiplying effect that took place. It's the "X" factor, as many people call it; the "je ne sais quoi" that makes a performer special and yet is difficult to pinpoint. The techniques we would be learning were the differences that make the difference; what separates the craftspeople from the masters.

Every morning at the crack of dawn we would do 30 minutes of yoga on the beach, eat breakfast, do a voice class, and then proceed to our Stage Presence class and do script work.

The voice class was remarkably like what I remembered from my university days—humming and tongue twisters. But this time,

I had Bob Fitch, a stage and screen veteran, right in my face, analyzing every sound coming out of my mouth. He was there to make sure we weren't phoning it in—that we were doing it right. He wouldn't let up and move on to the next person until he heard what he wanted to hear in terms of tone and quality.

After a few days of this regimen, it opened my ears. As I watched Fitch work with the other participants, I started to hear the differences in their voices. There was more presence and resonance coming from them. More importantly, I could hear it in my voice too. After years of knowing that voice work was something performers did, I was finally getting an experiential understanding of why we work on our voices.

From that point on, I made it a pre-show ritual to do the work and warm up my voice properly. To get it to the point where I can hear the difference and know that I'm sounding my best.

My goal in this chapter is to win you over to the idea that we can do more with our voices than we thought possible. I want you to care enough not only to try out some of the following suggestions but to keep at them for a period of 30 days.

Don't judge too soon. Give the processes some time and then measure to see how far you've come.

How the voice works

Everyone is familiar with the vocal chords, which are folds of tissue that vibrate when air is passed through them. What people don't often realize is that just like a guitar where the strings need the body of the guitar to make the sound fuller and louder, we have our own resonators—the chest, head, mouth, and nasal/mask area. In fact, the whole body is really a resonator. It's said that when someone loses a limb in an accident or amputation that the sound of their voice changes, which means we really do use our whole bodies to communicate.

Warming up your voice loosens up the resonators, allowing for deeper and richer tones. Why is that important? Evolutionarily, we tend to look to those with deeper, more resonant voices as having natural leadership qualities. The "alpha male" stereotype, whether you like it or not, does carry sway with our unconscious minds. We tend to respect the authority of people with more powerful voices as opposed to smaller, weaker ones.

Then there are the articulators, which are the tongue, teeth, and lips. These are what allow you to *pronounce words properly* (say that five times real fast). It's not unusual for people to mumble or be lazy with their elocution. In some industries—tech for one—there's specialist jargon that often includes compound multi-syllabic nouns (just like that one) that are difficult to pronounce. Doing an articulation exercise (which is basically a tongue twister) will improve how clearly the words come out of your mouth, making your content easier to understand.

Have you ever been on a call with a salesperson or customer service agent and you can't understand them? It's terribly frustrating. At a certain point, you just give up. That is obviously not engagement!

The articulation exercises we will share can help you be better understood and are the same kind of exercises that speech pathologists use to help people with a speech impediment. In fact, one of the performers who regularly attended the performer workshop I mentioned earlier, lost his very pronounced lisp after a year of applying these techniques.

Vocal elements

Volume

This is the simplest of the elements. This is how loudly or how quietly you talk. For the most part, people don't speak loudly enough to be heard. On a scale from 1 to 10, most people could afford to be bumped up a notch or two. Then there are people like me, who sometimes need to be reminded to use their inside voice. Anytime I'm passionate about something, my volume increases. If you're like me, it's good to monitor your volume. We don't want to repel those we're trying to engage by being overbearing with our voices. Typically, the recommendation is to mirror the volume you hear from the other person. This way, you match what's coming at you.

Tone

Tone is the scale of airy to edgy—airy being a whisper, with hardly any tone behind it, and full-on edginess being a strong nasal sound. On the low end, you have a harmless whisp of a voice, and on the opposite end, an aggressive, almost offensive sounding voice.

Depending on what you're speaking about, you'll want to aim for something between the two. Use more hushed tones when trying to soothe someone, and edgier tones for when you need to ramp up the tension. Creating a mixture between air and edge creates an interesting meld that is most pleasurable to the ear.

Pleasurable tones are more than an accident. Ever been to Vegas? The sounds of the slot machines when you hit the casino floor are carefully tuned to a tone that's been found to be likeable to the human ear. It's a pleasurable sound that reinforces the behavior of playing slots.

Humans can create pleasurable tones too. Think of a radio personality, a voiceover artist, or even a hypnotist. There's a certain sound you've come to expect from professional speakers and performers—it is the tone we like to hear.

Ironically, most people don't like the sound of their own voice when they hear recordings. But no matter how much you dislike the sound of your own voice, know that you can improve it and move your range into those more pleasing tones. We all can't have a radio voice, but we can sound better than our current baseline.

Pitch

Pitch is the note at which a voice typically resides. It's the place at which we're most comfortable. Even though we like staying at home base, it's good to vary your pitch when the right situations arise. If you're excited, let your voice get higher. If you need to be serious, drop your pitch to convey the mood of your topic.

Some people have naturally higher voices. If they're in authority positions, it may serve them to use a lower pitch when dealing with employees as a way to command more respect. If you're rapport building and looking to connect with others, it's recommended to use a pitch that is like their own. We like others that are like us. Adopting a similar pitch unconsciously bonds us to those who we are mirroring.

Modulation

Modulation is the variation in pitch—the hills and valleys of your voice; the melody of how you talk. On the low end of the modulation spectrum, you have monotone, sounds all of the same pitch—think classic "robot" voice. At the high end of the modulation spectrum is a kindergarten teacher trying to engage their class of five-year-olds. Modulation is important because of the contrast it creates. Remember: same is lame, so being monotone is a sure-fire way to put your listeners to sleep. Modulate to create interest and retain your listener's attention.

Intonation

Intonation is the rising, falling, or lack of movement in tone at the end of a sentence. When your tone rises at the end of a sentence, do you know what that is? That's right—it's a question.

When your tone remains the same at the end of a sentence, it's a statement.

If your tone goes down at the end of your sentence, it sounds like a command.

People who tend to use rising intonation at the end of every sentence sound like they're constantly asking questions. If you do this, you're undermining your own authority. When I hear people "uptalking," I'm constantly thinking, "Are you telling me or asking me?"

The command tone is very powerful but can come across as bossy if it's overused. The command tone carries assertive energy—the kind you need to make a dog obey. As a kid I could never get my dog to listen to me—I would say the right words, but I wasn't saying the words right.

Pace

Pace is the speed at which you speak. This is important in terms of rapport building as we tend to like people who speak at a pace similar to our own. Imagine if you will, the mismatch of two people with stereotypical rates of speech from Texas and from New York. The Texan's pace would be too slow for the New Yorker and, of course, the New Yorker would be speaking too fast for the Texan.

Speak at the same pace as your counterpart and you'll be laying the foundations for rapport and deeper connection. Never speak faster than your audience's ability to consume.

Fast-paced speech is typically more engaging than slow and plodding speech, yet if you're losing people because of your pace, it's all wasted energy. Watch your audience carefully—their body language will tell you volumes. If they look confused, slow down; if they look bored, pick up the pace.

By combining these elements in different ways, you'll create a myriad of effects that will bring focus to your ideas and move people unconsciously, just with the power of your voice. By varying the elements, you create contrast, which re-engages the ears (and minds) of your listeners.

Voice work

For those of you who've bought in and are ready to start making your voices sound better, I have some prescriptions for you.

1. Stretch your neck, shoulders, and jaw muscles before doing any mission-critical presentations. By stretching and releasing tension, you're loosening the "strings of the guitar," which creates a lower note. When you're relaxed, you'll also put your audience at ease.

2. Every day for the next 30 days, do some low humming while you're walking or driving. You want to hum at a pitch that's low, but not so low that you can't get any volume. Over time, this humming will bring your pitch down. It also warms you up before a speaking session.

3. Find several tongue twisters and practice saying them at the end of your humming warm-up. Like an athlete stretching their muscles, a speaker needs to do the same. One of my favorite warm-ups is saying the letters Q-U-Q-E, over and over again. It only takes 10–20 seconds before your cheeks are burning.

4. Another great articulating exercise is to read a passage from a book with a pencil between your teeth. The pencil makes it a lot more difficult to talk and to compensate you find yourself enunciating more prominently.

5. Grab a kids' book (I love to use books by Robert Munsch). Read each and every word to underline that word's meaning. So when you say "fiery," you say it with some airiness to make it sound more fiery. When you say "unfortunately," say it with a wah-wah tone. I think you get the idea. This makes for an animated and exciting reading, not unlike the over-modulating kindergarten teacher I mentioned earlier. While we would never actually speak like this, we want to practice emphasizing the words and their meaning so that when we're out in the world, a little bit of it sticks with us.

My goal is to open your eyes (and your ears) to the fact that we really do neglect our voices. Hopefully, you have a greater understanding of how you can improve your vocal engagement. If you would like to go deeper and explore how to be more engaging with your voice, reach out and we would be happy to connect you with one of our *Engagify* vocal coaches.

Chapter 18
Let's get physical

Do you talk with your hands? Ever since I was young, people have commented that I tend to rely on my hands when I speak. Some people speculated that it's due to my French heritage, while others thought I just had so much to say that I needed my hands to help out.

For some people, using their bodies to communicate comes more naturally than for others. Sometimes knowing that people are watching you—when you are making a presentation in front of a group, for example—can really impact how you move.

When practicing public speaking in school, I remember feeling awkward and not knowing what to do with my hands. It was only when I relaxed and immersed myself in the presentation that my body language started looking more natural.

The way we move when we interact is inherently tied to the quality of our communication. A study from 1967 found that when an incongruent message is being communicated regarding feelings and attitudes, we tend to rely on the body language and facial expressions the most. In the study, Albert Mehrabian found that 55% of the communicated message relied on seeing the communicator to decipher this incongruent message. In other words, by not tapping into our bodies as an instrument of communication, we are losing credibility that would otherwise make our message easier to receive and understand.

(Note: The Mehrabian study is often misquoted. The important part is when an "incongruent message is being communicated regarding feelings and attitudes." This study cannot be universally applied to all contexts.)

Physicality does a lot of the heavy lifting when we speak. Our words can be deceptive, but our bodies tell the real story. As ex-NFL player, speaker trainer, and actor Bo Eason says, "Mother Nature never lies." Because our actions speak louder than our words, it's up to us to ensure congruence between the two.

Much like our voices, we often overlook the persuasive power of our physicality.

If you told someone that they need to be more physical, the first thing many people might think of is physical comedy. Black and white clips from The Three Stooges and the stunts of Buster Keaton instantly come to mind. While these performers were masters at their craft, that's not what's required for added engagement.

Humans are lazy by nature—we have a tendency to take the path of least resistance. As a survival mechanism, we'll opt for the lowest calorie expenditure whenever possible. This has resulted in a society (in my opinion) that does things half-heartedly. If you look at the way people move, there's a lack of intention. There's no decisiveness in the movements. In order to communicate more effectively and drive engagement, our movements need to become more meaningful and intentional.

Magicians know a thing or two about attracting the eye and—more importantly—not attracting the eye, or mis-directing attention.

When magicians first learn magic and perform basic sleight of hand, they start to develop a sense of what people are watching. It often begins with a basic coin vanish known as the French Drop. This is when the magician appears to grab a coin from one hand with the other hand, but, in fact, the coin remains in the first hand.

In my case, I would practice in the mirror for hours on end, watching my own movements and trying to make a feint look natural. Then I would perform these sleights in front of family or friends to see if I could pull off the trick without anyone spotting the deception. Early on I would get caught, but soon I discovered which movements aroused suspicion, and which ones went under the radar. With time and experience, magicians come to know what people will watch and what they won't.

Focusing an audience's attention with your body language can be summed up by this figure.

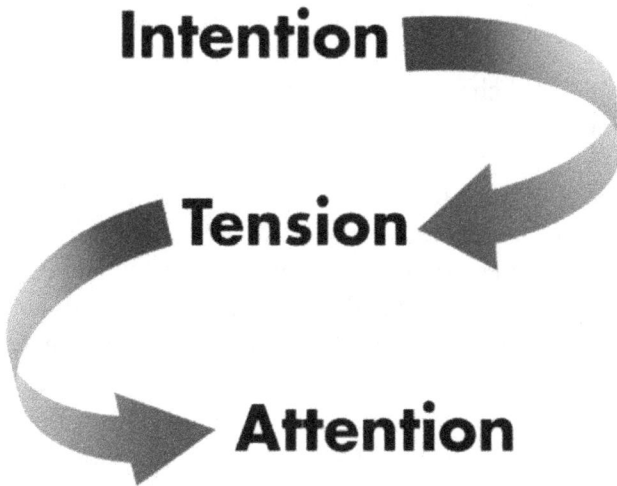

Intention

Tension

Attention

For a magician, the intention in a coin trick is to have the audience watch one hand and not the other. That intention creates physical tension in the hand that supposedly is holding the coin. This hand is raised higher (to eye level), giving it greater importance. By comparison, the hand containing the covertly concealed coin is dangling by the magician's side, loose and relaxed.

The hand that vanishes the coin is clenched tightly—almost appearing to crush the coin—before it is shown to have disappeared. Tension in our actions attracts the eye because there is intention behind it.

If you want to focus someone's attention on your message, you need to embody your intentions physically.

I used to be very cynical about the idea that a mere thought can affect an outcome. I'm not talking about The Secret here, I'm talking about a straight-line connection between how you think about something and how your body responds to that thought.

For a number of years I studied Aikido. For those of you who aren't familiar with Aikido, it's a Japanese martial art whose name loosely translates as the "way of harmony." The "ki" in Aikido refers to what might be better known to some people as the Chinese equivalent "Chi," or "life force." Initially, I wasn't too into the "mystical" side of this, because I didn't understand it. Our Sensei (teacher) would challenge us to harness our ki to make us better practitioners.

In Aikido, you learn to do shoulder rolls to help you fall without hurting yourself. To conserve your momentum, it's important to roll smoothly. If any of us was having issues, Sensei would give us something to think about. "Pretend that you have a bowl full of water right at your Obi (belt) knot—don't spill the water." At the time, you'd be thinking, okay... interesting coaching suggestion; but then you would try it and your roll would noticeably improve. Bringing the intention of not spilling the water resulted in a more effective outcome in the performance of the roll. The thought created the right conditions in the body to execute the move properly.

Another Aikido example is the unbendable arm, in which two individuals of a similar build face one another. Person A puts their right arm palm up on the left shoulder of Person B. Person A is instructed to clench their fist and tense their arm to resist the pressure. Person B places their hands on top of Person A's elbow joint and pulls down while leaning forward, thus bending the arm of Person A. This is expected because B has the mechanical advantage.

Next, A is told to keep their hand open (rather than clenched) and let the ki flow through their arm. They are told to extend energy through their arm, picturing the arm as a 40-foot-long fire hose that's shooting energy from the end of it. Person B once again tries to bend the arm of A, only this time, the arm won't bend. The look on Person B's face is priceless because they feel that their strength has been sapped, while A, on the other hand, isn't even sure how they're accomplishing the feat.

Here's the secret...

It's not just how you think about it, but how your body understands the mind's instructions. In the first scenario, Person A tenses his arm, but in doing so, engages both the bicep and the triceps, which is counterproductive because those two muscles are on opposite sides of the joint. The mechanics of the situation require the triceps to do the work. In the second scenario, that's exactly what happens. The imagery of the 40-foot fire hose and the visualization of the flow of energy was enough to tell the body exactly what it needed to do (engage only the triceps); only, instead of precise physical instructions, it was the intention—the idea—that brought it to reality.

What is the intention you take into your presentations and interactions? Is it specific? Do you embody that intention? Start to experiment by concentrating on bringing one thing with you into your interaction or presentation. Are you trying to energize your audience? Inspire them? Connect with them? Depending on what you concentrate on, your resulting movements and actions will vary. Play with this, trying different intentions.

Create a sense of danger

Neuroscience tells us that humans are visually stimulated. The optic nerve is directly connected to the limbic system. This means that our lizard brains, responsible for fight or flight, are keenly aware of what we see. From an evolutionary point of view, this is important because we need to be scanning for danger in order to survive to see another day.

Years ago, when I was still performing magic on stage, I would often walk right out into the audience to find volunteers at various parts of the show. As I stepped off the stage, I could immediately sense how uncomfortable people were at the prospect of being asked to come up on stage. The closer I got to someone, the more they'd squirm. I would hear murmurs of "Don't pick me!" It made me feel like a predator on the prowl. At one point in the show, I would intentionally move through the crowd as if I was hunting for my next victim. Over the sound system you would hear the *Jaws* theme song playing, which added to the sense of impending doom.

Do you think anyone took their eyes off me while this was happening? Not a chance. When we see someone, or something move like a dangerous animal it's very difficult to look away. If you found yourself inside the tiger enclosure at the zoo, you would be on high alert.

People who are very connected to and in tune with their bodies can give off that same dangerous vibe. The way that athletes move, and their posterior chain (the entire backside) is engaged can give the impression of a lion on the prowl. Actors work on this same thing to create that animal magnetism. After meeting Sean Connery for the first time, James Bond producer Cubby Broccoli watched Connery from his office window as he was leaving the audition. Cubby marveled at Connery's confidence and sexually charged "panther-like" strut. The producers were so impressed with Connery's physicality that they instantly decided to give him the role of the English spy, even though he was from Scotland.

In my career, I've worked on my own physicality with various teachers. One of the exercises that performance consultant Bob Fitch taught me was walk back and forth across a stage, employing different body leads. A body lead is an area of your body that seems to drive your movement forward. Some people walk with their head leading, others with their chest, their feet, or even their crotch! Each of the different body leads produces a different look and feel. The purpose of the exercise was to find the walk that looked best on me, that would create the most stage presence. To the lay person, it's bizarre to think that someone might actually work on their walk (unless you're a runway model, perhaps). These are exactly the layers that, when combined with other elements from this book, cultivate the charisma that drives engagement and creates fascination in the people you meet.

I have a trade show presenter friend named Amy McWhirter. She's an ultra-professional, classy emcee and presenter. Not long after meeting her, I noticed something about the way she moves. She has an unmistakable grace to her. Her movements are so smooth and her lines so interesting that I just had to go up to her and ask, "You've done ballet, haven't you?" She kind of blushed and admitted that she'd been dancing all her life. That kind of work and dedication shows up in your performance. Does this mean you have to dedicate the next 20 years of your life to dance? No, of course not. But here are a few ideas to get you on the path to optimizing the use of your body as a communication tool.

Awareness

As with anything you learn, the first step is merely awareness— not only awareness of what kind of emphasis you bring to your message through gestures, facial expressions, and energy—but awareness of how others move.

Years ago, my wife dragged me to a Michael Bublé concert. This was before he was as famous as he is now. I wasn't too big into the jazz "standards," but once I started watching the concert, I was mesmerized by how Bublé moved on stage. He would slide around the stage in his leather shoes and strike the most interesting poses as he belted out the lyrics to his songs. I was so taken with his performance that after the concert, I started writing notes about what made it such a great show. I advise you to do what I did: be on the lookout for people who are interesting to watch and try to figure out what it is about the way they move that intrigues you; if appropriate, emulate those movements in your own life.

Play bigger

Don't be afraid to take up more space. When performers are on stage, their job is to fill up the stage with their presence. Keeping an open posture says to the world that you're ready to engage. Years before Amy Cuddy hit the scene with her research on power posing, performers have known that people are attracted to the arms-stretched-out-wide pose.

In my own work on stages and in trade show booths, I can quickly measure the impact of playing bigger and taking up more space. When the body is angled in such a way that more people are seeing the expressive parts of you (face and torso), there's a better chance they'll be interested in what you're sharing and they'll stop to watch. Another one of my mentors—a man named David Stahl— once said to me, "Play to the crowd you want, not to the crowd you have." What he meant was to not only engage with the people who are standing and watching you but also to those areas where a crowd hasn't developed yet. The only way you can accomplish this is by keeping an open posture and playing big.

Tune in

Lastly, get in tune with your body. Develop a better understanding of where your body is in space—a concept called proprioception. This awareness of where your body is will help you get your body to where it needs to be.

I highly recommend taking a martial arts class to better understand not only your body but the energy flowing within it. My favorite, of course, is Aikido, but find one that suits you. Don't like combat? Try some Tai Chi or Qi-Gong. Of course, yoga and dance are also great options to connect to your body.

Bo Eason swears by standing on rocks. He knows that if he can feel connected to the ground, his body will respond in the way that he needs it to. Get yourself a rock about the size of a bar of soap and stand on the rock (with your feet bare or in socks). Make it hurt a bit and really dig your foot into the rock. When you take your foot off the rock and back onto the floor, you can feel your foot spreading out, providing stability and connection to the ground. Repeat with the other foot. (This practice is more common than you might think and can be seen in some elite gyms across the U.S.)

This exercise gives people a rootedness that changes the way that they move and how people perceive them.

If you want to move in ways that people find fascinating and get more of your message across through your body language, take a lesson from actors, dancers, and athletes, bring an intention into your presentation, play big, and stand on rocks!

Chapter 19
Virtual engagement

If you mentioned *virtual meetings* before the year 2020, chances are few would have known what you were talking about. (Platforms like Skype, Zoom, and FaceTime had been around for some time, but we tended to refer to them as *video calls*.)

Then the COVID-19 pandemic hit and everything changed. Without the ability to meet face-to-face (in-person), virtual meetings became the next best thing.

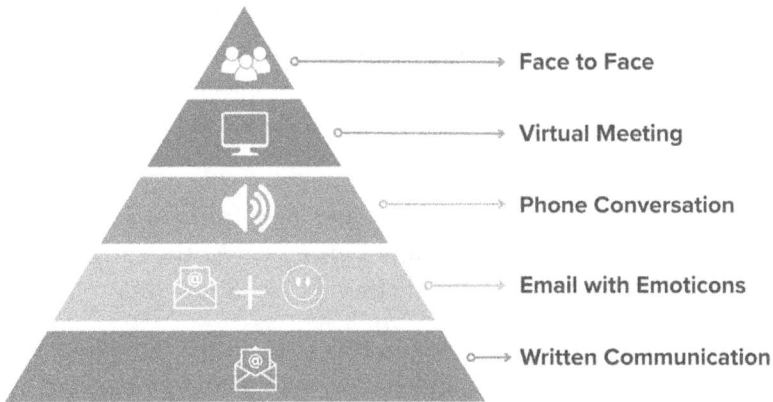

Face to Face

Virtual Meeting

Phone Conversation

Email with Emoticons

Written Communication

Written communication can communicate ideas but not in real time. It also lacks tone. You may have experienced this if you have ever attempted to make a joke in an email and the humor was misinterpreted by the recipient.

That's why emoji serve a purpose. Most people believe that emoticons are just for texting. Those same people might be surprised to learn that C-suite executives have embraced emojis as a way to add meaning and context but also to save time. The "winky face" has successfully conveyed the tongue-in-cheek tone required to joke or poke fun in a written context.

Phone conversations have the tone that's lacking from written words; we can hear not only what is said, but how it's said. While being an improvement over written communication, it lacks the visual cues that make in-person interactions so effective. We can't see the person's face, see their body language, and feel their general presence.

While on the phone tone of voice can be heard, the technology that simplifies our voices so it can be efficiently transmitted over phone lines hasn't changed for a very long time. Our voices are compressed on the phone and the richness of sound that's possible with in-person conversation is lost. It's a step up from writing for sure, but still not the ideal.

Virtual meetings or video calls allow us to not only hear a person in real time but to see them as well. The technology simulates face-to-face interactions but it doesn't duplicate them. As the saying goes, "No matter how much you click from place to place, you'll never replace face-to-face."

Virtual meetings are the highest and best form of interaction we have when geographic limitations exist. (At the time of this writing, holograms are still only found in sci-fi movies.)

The world was slowly moving in this virtual direction when the COVID-19 pandemic hit and forced our hand. For business to continue, companies had to adapt and adopt this new medium of communication. As it turns out, some buyers prefer this online process. They would no longer have to "entertain" a salesperson, give them coffee, chit chat, and build rapport. Virtual meetings can be tighter and more efficient. If one party needs to leave, they're just a mouse click away from doing so. Unfortunately, this same detachment means that online-only relationships are rarely as strong or as powerful as those created in person.

Now that the world is accustomed to this mode of communication, virtual meetings will continue to be an effective tool of interaction but not without its limitations.

Trouble reading the room

The brain is such an amazing tool. Humans are social animals, and for centuries we've evolved to be empathetic and to unconsciously pick up on certain signals—instinctively knowing how to act and what to do. But picking up on these signals is not so easy when we are connecting via Zoom.

Without being in the same room as others and breathing the same air, we have a difficult time picking up on those subtleties that would otherwise cue us, both consciously and unconsciously, as to what they are attempting to communicate. Whether it's a noise filter or an insufficiently sensitive microphone, you may not pick up on a labored exhale, for example. Normally, you would know that your counterpart's patience has run out and you should wrap up your presentation; but you didn't hear that breath cue, so you continue selling to a frustrated buyer.

Because we aren't talking to a live human who's right in front of us—just an image of one on screen—we lack the empathy we'd normally have. This makes the connection we create in an interaction tenuous.

One of the biggest frustrations voiced by the people we train in virtual engagement is that they don't have a trustworthy feedback loop. They're sending out a message, but they don't have the necessary feedback to measure the effectiveness or quality of that communication. For example, you know you sound clear when you speak to someone in-person, but online, your mic could be making you sound garbled or annoying. Maybe there's an echo bouncing off your desk or maybe your mic isn't the best quality, but unless you record yourself and check these things before your meeting, you'll never know how you are being perceived.

All the engagement skills in the world are wasted in a virtual meeting if your sound is a turn-off and your image is grainy.

Dark rooms and nose jobs

Putting your best foot forward in the virtual meeting space requires more know-how than an in-person meeting—know-how and some decent equipment.

Many Zoom participants are backlit and hard to see. Their webcams may be at a strange angle—either too high (looking down) or too low (looking up the nose). Webcams vary in quality and many don't handle light well, creating grainy pictures. If people can't see you properly, they'll have more trouble fully understanding your message. If what they see is hard on their eyes (like a virtual background that's ghosting all around you as parts of your body randomly disappear), they might even tune out all together.

Distractions reign supreme

If you've ever spoken to someone at a party who's clearly looking for someone else to talk to instead of you, you have some idea of how frustrating it can be to try and communicate with someone who isn't present.

In a virtual call, that person is now taking a meeting on the same dopamine-spiking device that they use for playing video games, watching movies, looking at social media, and doing online shopping. The entire internet is at their beck and call, and you have no idea if they're actually watching you or are off-tasking.

If they're working from home, the potential for distraction is even worse.[1] The home environment offers a laundry list (literally!) of possible distractions—a dog barking, a courier at the door, a young child demanding attention, and yes, even the laundry.

Studies show that in a video conference call with a number of employees, over 60% of attendees are emailing, eating, exercising, and generally splitting their attention with other tasks.[2]

Maybe it's a good thing it's hard to read the room—we might be mortified to know who is (and who is not) actually paying attention.

At *Engagify*, we've been selling virtually since long before it was called *virtual selling*. It began as a way to augment our phone conversations with visual aids. We used a service called Meeting Burner and then moved to Skype shortly after. My slide presentations always included animations, and I loved bringing them to life, so I kept looking for new and better ways to paint a picture of our services.

Then we discovered Zoom and fully embraced the platform about five years before COVID-19 hit in early 2020, putting us ahead of the curve of later adopters.

Being comfortable with your meeting platform is such a big part of a successful interaction. If you know your platform and can troubleshoot and recover from any situation, you can relax and concentrate on your engagement skills in the moment.

---

[1] SHRM, *How to reduce digital distractions at work*, Society for Human Resource Management (2019). Available from www.shrm.org/topics-tools/news/technology/how-to-reduce-digital-distractions-work [accessed May 25, 2025].

[2] R. S. Oeppen, G. Shaw, and P. A. Brennan, "Human factors recognition at virtual meetings and video conferencing: How to get the best performance from yourself and others" in *The British Journal of Oral & Maxillofacial Surgery*, 58 (6), 643–646 (2020). doi: 10.1016/j.bjoms.2020.04.046.

A low bar

Ninety-five percent of people who enter a virtual meeting do nothing in terms of preparation. They go from working on their computers straight into a meeting. There's no forethought given to how they look on screen, their lighting or sound, or even to their mental and physical state. The result is a flat, uninspired, boring interaction. No wonder there's Zoom fatigue—people are tired of being bored!

The good news is that those who care to make an effort are rewarded. They're looked upon as a breath of fresh air.

Since we started training sales teams in virtual engagement, we see every call with a potential client as an audition. Our virtual interactions must be off-the-charts better than what they would typically experience. We must look better, sound better, and be more interesting than anything they encounter in the rest of their day. After completing a call with us, we want them to think, "Boy, I wish our salespeople were just a little more like that!"

What's at stake?

So what? Who cares? Why does it matter?

If you're managing a team virtually, your overall employee engagement will correlate very closely with the engagement you get during your virtual calls. Employee retention, productivity, and overall team health can and will be affected by the level of engagement you have in your weekly calls.

Do your employees feel exhausted after a Zoom meeting? What if they could be invigorated instead? What could they achieve?

Selling in the age of Zoom is a challenge for many salespeople. They no longer feel that the force of their personality can win the day. They've lost their superpower. If their prospects aren't engaged in the meeting, what are the chances that the deal will progress? By improving virtual engagement skills, they can learn to close faster, win bigger—and do so more of the time.

Even if you don't use virtual meetings for business, you may be using this medium to stay connected to friends and family. If that's the case, your online experiences will be deeper and richer, just by following the suggestions at the end of this chapter.

Increasing your virtual engagement

The first step to increasing your virtual meeting power is to commit to getting better. If you truly care about getting through to your audience—to ensure that they get the best experience from your online interaction—you need to go beyond just turning on your camera. You must care enough to go to the trouble of doing the extra work. For salespeople, this is more of a no-brainer than for other folks because they'll be rewarded with commissions for their extra effort.

Get equipped to engage

No matter how engaging you are as a person, if you can't be seen and heard properly, all your soft skills will be good for nothing. In our trainings, we often quote a line from the Hippocratic Oath: "First do no harm." If your sound and video aren't offending your meeting counterpart, you're already in a better position to build from than those who haven't taken the effort to ensure the quality of their technology.

Up your camera game

Most webcams installed as a device on your computer cost only about $0.30 to manufacture. Few are of a high resolution that handle light well. This can result in blurry, fuzzy images. Often, the white balance is off and the colors won't look true to life. In our virtual engagement training, we recommend obtaining a

182 | Engage First

standalone camera. You can get better quality video and better camera angles because the camera isn't embedded in your screen.

Sound like a pro

Most offices are full of hard, flat surfaces that produce echoes and bad sound. We are big fans of capturing sound at the source and using a lavalier mic so the sound doesn't have to travel and bounce around too much before your computer picks up the signal. You may also want to look at soundproofing your area. Room dividers, drapes, or carpet all work to absorb sound and deaden the room. Experiment by recording yourself with different configurations and find out which sounds the best.

Curate your background

Backgrounds can be distracting. If people place themselves in front of a bookshelf, I often find myself trying to read the spines of the books I see. We have control of our backgrounds in that we decide where we will situate ourselves. Curate your background either by moving your camera and trying different locations or angles, or by moving or arranging what's behind you. For example, you can create interest by shining lights on the wall.

If you're a photographer, you're probably familiar with the Law of Thirds. This is a rule in composition that divides your frame into nine equal boxes. The subject of the shot should be either at the intersection of these lines or running along one of the vertical lines. Once you understand this principle, you'll see it used in movies, photographs, and art. Using this principle as a guideline, find an arrangement that's attractive and interesting, but not distracting. You're looking for a way to frame yourself and make you the focal point.

Play to the camera

Virtual meetings are so popular because they're the closest thing we have to a face-to-face interaction. But there are some drawbacks that need to be understood. One of them is that we tend to look at the screen and not the camera. We're wired to give eye contact to the people we speak with, and yet when we look them in the "eyes" on screen, we're actually casting our gaze down, away from the camera—the result being that we don't appear to be making eye contact at all. People who avoid eye contact are often seen as shifty or untrustworthy.

By doing what we instinctively want to do, we're undermining the building blocks necessary for creating successful and lasting relationships. To combat this tendency, we need to remind ourselves to focus on the camera when we speak. In our virtual engagement training course, we instruct students to make a little arrow out of a Post-it note and stick it to the bottom of the camera to remind them to look up.

Every time you're speaking you should be directing your energy and focus on that lens. You must connect to that camera as if it's a person. One of my students created a collage of faces with a hole in it to fit over the camera lens. When you look at those paper faces, not only are you looking at the camera, but you're reminded of the people on the other side of the lens.

When we do have someone in the room, our energy is increased because we're affected by their energy. This gives our communication extra punch and makes for a livelier conversation. However, on a virtual call, we're often in a room by ourselves. This lowers the energy, and we may end up coming across as flat. Though I can't quite explain it, the webcam just seems to suck energy from the meeting.

Give 33% extra

We teach our students to amp up their performance energy by 33%. That might sound like a lot, but there are a few things to consider. First, what you think is appropriate energy isn't as much as you think it is. Then the camera tends to kill some of that energy as well.

Second, with no one around you to naturally pull energy from, you'll have less pop than usual. So just to be perceived at the level you *think* you're at, you have to overshoot your performance energy by 33%.

Be present

We've discussed all the distractions that our counterpart is facing and how we must up our engagement game to keep their attention on us, but we must remember to stay present ourselves.

The more you focus on the present moment and tune into the other party, the more you can influence their behavior so they start cueing off of you. Be authentic, sincere, and let your empathy come through in your words and actions. To hone your virtual presence, you must first be present. This skill is such a rarity in today's world, you'll stand out and be noticed if you're able to master it.

In summary

Virtual engagement can be very counter intuitive—from not knowing how you actually sound to the listener on the other end, to giving the illusion of eye contact by looking at the camera lens rather than the faces on screen. These concepts may be foreign to people who've never had a reason to consider them before. But as remote work and virtual meetings find a permanent place in the business landscape, those who adapt and learn to engage in the virtual world will stand head and shoulders above the competition.

CONCLUSION

Chapter 20
The breakfast of champions

If you've ever played with a microphone and a sound system and accidentally passed the mic in front of the speaker, you know what feedback is. It's the ear-piercing squeal that comes rushing out of the speaker. The shrill noise is the result of the sound being amplified by the sound system over and over again in a continuous loop, or a feedback loop.

A feedback loop starts with a behavior or action (walking in front of the speaker with a live mic). This is followed by a reaction (the squealing sound) and then a modification of the behavior (turning the mic off or not walking in front of the speaker).

Feedback loops are in play in every aspect of our lives. They shape our behavior. When it comes to engagement, the most engaging people I've met in my lifetime have been entertainers. When you think about it, it makes perfect sense. They're a product of their environments. The way they act, speak, and behave has been shaped by the reactions their audiences have given them in real time. This loop is tight—feedback is immediate. As a comedian, you tell a joke, and the audience either laughs or doesn't. If they don't laugh, you need to tell the joke better, rewrite the joke, or get a new joke. Over time, both your material gets better and so do you as a performer.

For people not in the entertainment or speaking industry—those who do not play to an audience—the feedback loop is much slower. The timeline can sometimes be months instead of seconds. For salespeople, it might be the entire length of the sales cycle; with feedback only coming when they eventually learn whether they closed a sale or not. For some people, feedback might not come until their annual review—and by the time that rolls around, they've been doing things right or wrong for so long, it's often difficult to implement the suggestions and the coaching.

Ken Blanchard, co-author of the book *Raving Fans*, says that "Feedback is the breakfast of champions."[1] He's right, we need feedback to grow in the areas we need to develop.

Tight feedback loops are necessary for faster learning and implementation. Not long ago, I was tasked with creating a 30-second introduction video for one of our clients. We've had a long relationship with this company, and they often lean on us to create content and act as an ambassador for their organization. In this instance, they needed a punchy, peppy video to grab people's attention and convey the message they wanted to communicate. I told them that this wouldn't be a problem. "I can do peppy," I said.

What followed was a series of 25 or more 30-second clips of me recording myself again and again… and again. What I realized each time I reviewed a clip, was that what I thought was peppy was actually coming off as flat. I needed to give even more energy than I thought was necessary. I would record that 30-second clip, and then watch the entire 30 seconds. Then I would try it again and again, tweaking my delivery until I reached the desired level of "peppiness."

Watching video footage is an excellent tool for learning exactly how you're being perceived. The camera never lies. Magicians who practice in front of a mirror sometimes develop a bad habit of

---

[1] K. Blanchard and S. Bowles, *Raving Fans: A revolutionary approach to customer service*. William Morrow, 1993.

blinking when they perform a certain move. They want the move to be invisible, so they trick themselves into not seeing it. This doesn't work with a video camera, and doesn't work before an audience either. The camera never lies.

To engage with others, we must not only send and receive communication, we must also understand that our audience is not always receiving what we think they are. Sometimes their experience can be far from what we intended and they receive far less of our message than we hoped—but sometimes their experience can far exceed anything we ever imagined.

From the time I was 18 years old until I was about 24, I worked summers doing magic at a resort-town restaurant. My job was to swoop in after an order was taken and entertain the guests until their food arrived. It was a careful balance of respecting the customers' dining experience while offering the option of enhancing their time there with a tableside interactive magic show. It added a unique feature to the atmosphere and many guests would come back wanting to see a new magic trick.

With every table, I learned more of what to do and what not to do. Every night I experimented with my initial approach to each table, thinking about the size of my smile, my opening line, how to tactfully interrupt a conversation and introduce myself, how to explain what I was proposing to show them. Even with the promise of an entertaining experience, diners sometimes turned it down—much to the dismay of any children present.

One evening after closing time, I was finishing my complimentary pizza (a bonus, in addition to my tips and fees) when Teen, the restaurant owner, sat down with me. She asked me if I remembered the family of three I had entertained at one particular table earlier in the evening. I did—it was a mother and her two kids—a boy about nine years old and a girl about 11 or 12. I recalled it being a fun family to interact with but otherwise nothing out of the ordinary from my perspective. They had been just one of 20 or more tables I had entertained over the course of the evening.

Teen then explained that they had been at the restaurant exactly one year earlier to the day—only, at that time they had been a family of four. This year the father was missing. She told me how that this family had a tradition: every year on the last day of their stay in the park, they would have a meal at the restaurant. After their last meal the previous year, they drove the 100 kilometers home and unpacked the car. Tragically, as they unloaded the car on their driveway, the father had a heart attack and died.

One year later, they returned to their traditional summer vacation spot, minus one member of the family. As they always did, they went for their last meal at the restaurant before returning home, and as they had the year before, they got to experience some tableside magic.

Upon leaving the restaurant, they had made a special mention to Teen to thank me for performing so they could re-visit fond memories of the last day when their husband and father was still in their lives. I was floored when I heard what had happened and reflected on how special that moment must have been for them. I hadn't done anything different from my usual interactions, but the impact of those moments was enormous given the circumstances and the filter through which they were experiencing the moment.

If only we knew the impact our interactions truly have. I suspect that you yourself have profoundly influenced others far beyond what you could ever believe. If we knew—if we could better understand the consequences of our actions—we would modify our behaviors and do more (or less) of the things that get positive results. Knowing that our interactions matter and can change people's thoughts and actions for the better, can inspire us to do better.

Growing up, I was head over heels in love with my passion: magic. I read every book my school library had on the subject, and every Christmas and birthday I would get magic sets and tricks as gifts. Of course, I idolized Houdini and looked at his life as a guide to my own. I even wore a handcuff key around my neck and would rub it for good luck. In studying Houdini, I learned that he was a teetotaler. As a kid I had to look up the meaning of this word, and I learned that it meant he never drank alcohol. Then and there, I decided that I would do the same thing.

During my freshmen year of high school—or grade nine, as we call it in Canada—the small class sizes at the school in my tiny hometown meant I was pretty much a shoo-in to make the varsity volleyball team. As a short, left-handed kid, I was a good fit for the position of setter. The only other setter on the team was also shorter than average but was looked up to as a leader by the rest of the team, in addition to being popular with the girls in the school. He even had a cool name: Jason Guy. Jason and I would warm up together during practices and games, and despite our age difference (he was a senior) and social status in the school, we were connected through volleyball.

One night, I was at a house party just down the street from my place. Small-town life didn't offer much in the way of constructive activities for teenagers; parties and underage drinking were the main source of entertainment. That night, I recall being bombarded with peer pressure to have a beer. I kept saying no—standing my ground in honor of my long-dead-and-gone magic hero.

"Have a beer!"

"No thanks."

"C'mon—just one!"

"No, I'm good thanks."

On and on—until finally I heard a voice say, "If Anders doesn't want to drink, he doesn't have to drink." It was Jason Guy.

Instantly the pressure subsided. The man at the top of the totem pole, a senior and one of the most popular guys in the school had spoken. Nobody pressured me to drink again for the rest of the night—or even the rest of that year. Someone choosing to speak up and engage in the situation made my first year easier, and as a result, the rest of my time in high school easier. To this day, he probably has no idea how a few well-timed words made a world of difference for me at a time when I really needed it.

So, as you can see, I've been on both ends of an interaction that—at first glance—seems fairly mundane and innocuous, yet the effects that are created are much farther reaching. We can never truly know the full impact that our interactions have, but knowing the potential for making positive change in the lives of others is inspiring and we should use that knowledge as encouragement to keep on engaging.

When you really connect with someone—in a conversation, a prospecting call, or in your travels—know that you aren't the only one benefitting from the good feelings that come with the interaction—the other person is too. You're changing their body chemistry, pumping up the oxytocin, and making them feel connected. Every interaction you have is setting the butterfly effect in motion, and once in a while—like my tableside magic performance for a widow and her two kids—you're lucky enough to learn the real impact of what you're doing. So keep on doing it.

Just like Babe Ruth, you've got to swing for the fences every single time. Do your best work and be present in every conversation, performance, and presentation.

My friend David Aiken (known as The Checkerboard Guy) is a juggler. He once told me about an occasion when he was street performing on a gray, rainy Vancouver day for a tiny crowd of eight people. Now, many street performers might just pack it in because the size of the hat (the money collected at the end of a show) would be too small to warrant getting soaked in the rain. But David thought that if the crowd was game, he was too, and they'd make it a show to remember. As it turns out, a cruise ship talent agent was in the audience that day, which is how The Checkerboard Guy started working on cruise ships. Every time out, you give it your all.

So how do we give it our all when it comes to engagement?

Be prepared.

Be prepared to give it your all. Don't "phone it in"—care about each and every interaction. If you're doing a presentation for your company, rehearse it. If you're going into a big sales meeting, roleplay the encounter. Know what you're going to say before you have to say it.

The biggest difference between professionals and amateurs in any field is the amount of time and effort they put into their craft. If you're meeting people virtually, what are you doing to be prepared? Do you use a virtual meeting checklist?

Be unique

Another way of taking greater care in your interactions and increasing the chances that you'll impact someone else's life is to bring a sense of uniqueness to every situation. What do I mean by uniqueness?

An actor learns the lines to a play and rehearses them hundreds of times before they perform in front of an audience. And though it's the 300th time for the actor, it's the first time that the audience has heard the actor say those lines. Actors call this the "illusion of the first time"—that is, creating a specialness about what you're doing. What would make it memorable and unique—like The Checkerboard Guy's show in the rain? How could you come together with your audience, the people at your work, or your potential customers to co-create an "event" that would make people glad they were there? When you can bring this sense of uniqueness and originality, you'll be remembered long term.

Be present

Besides being prepared and unique in your presentation, being present and in the moment can ensure that your interactions will have a profound effect. This allows you to be who you need to be for any given audience or group of people.

In Olivia Fox Cabane's book *The Charisma Myth*, she contends that individuals are not born with charisma, but that they can cultivate it. She asserts that it's a combination of three characteristics: warmth, presence, and power—but that only two out of the three are necessary in order to be charismatic. One example she cites is that of Steve Jobs, who was present and powerful, but not known for being a warm-and-fuzzy kind of guy. Another example is Bill Clinton, who's a perfect three out of three. He's warm and likable, and his presence is off the charts. Some say that when he speaks to a crowd, every person feels like they are in a one-to-one conversation. Not only does he possess presence and warmth, as a former president of the United States, he checks the power box easily.

We often live either in the past (thinking about what we shoulda, coulda, or woulda done) or the future (fretting and worrying about what is to come). Rarely do we come across an individual who's truly in the moment during the time that we spend with them. It happens so infrequently that individuals who live in the moment stick out in our memories. They teach us the value of pouring ourselves into whatever we're doing while we're doing it.

In summary

If you prepare, make your presentation unique, and are fully present, you'll find that the effects of your interactions far exceed expectations—both for you and the individuals you interact with. Occasionally, you might even hear about how you've made people feel and how your words and actions have positively affected them. This knowledge will drive you forward, giving you the positive feedback you need to continue engaging and making your presence felt.

Start with the end in mind

Congratulations! You've done what very few people actually do—you've finished a book. Doesn't seem like a big deal until you consider that 24% of Americans haven't read a book in the past year, let alone finished one. Not only that, but even Pulitzer Prize-winning books are often abandoned. According to Kobo, the eBook version of Donna Tartt's *The Goldfinch* was only finished by 44% of people who started it. While this book is not of that award-winning caliber, it does mean a lot that you've come this far. Give yourself a pat on the back for finishing what you start.

The key though, isn't just reading a non-fiction book and learning a few things here and there. It's about applying the skills and techniques taught within it. While some of the tools presented in this book can be cultivated by merely increasing your awareness and observing how you interact, others require a certain amount of dedication and practice.

Where to start?

No doubt, some of the topics in this book resonate more with you than others. This might be because you're already good at that particular skill or because you're well acquainted with the problem through past experience. I wish there was a prescription I could offer—a step-by-step process to overhaul your engagement skills—but everyone is different and has different strengths and weaknesses. I can, however, give you a framework to help you start your journey.

One thing at a time

As mentioned earlier, we're only able to be consciously aware of five, plus or minus two, things at one time. If I had you close your eyes right now and started asking you detailed questions about the color of the certain objects in the room, how many pieces of paper were on the table and so on, you would probably be embarrassed by how many of the things in your immediate surroundings you're not aware of. The same is true for how you approach the skills in this book. So, it's best to think of them as layers that you'll apply, one at a time, to what you're already doing.

In grade school when giving a presentation during class, something as simple as giving eye contact to your audience can be challenging at first, especially when you would much rather keep your head down and read your cue cards. But with practice, keeping your head up becomes second nature. If you're someone who does any public speaking, you probably don't even think about giving eye contact to your audience because once mastered, this kind of skill is applied unconsciously. This allows you to use that available mental bandwidth to add another layer to your presentation.

To this day, I go into an event with an intention. I pick a certain area to focus on. On top of the magic I may be performing (with moves and tools to use secretly), the script I've memorized, and the experience I want to create, I'll focus on improving one area and I use the remaining mental bandwidth to bring special attention to that one part of my performance. It's through specific focus and intention that depth and texture can be brought to a performance.

Don't be tempted to change more than one thing at a time. As much as you want to get results, adding too many things at once is a recipe for disaster. First, you won't be able to split-test this new element effectively. Only by adding one element at a time, can you get the feedback you need to judge whether or not you're getting any significant results. To evaluate: did you do it right in the first place? Did the other party respond in a favorable way? Adding one additional new skill or element is the way to go; then you can refine your technique and vary your approach to seek the improvements you're looking to gain.

The other danger of changing too much at once is that you run the risk of becoming overwhelmed. We learned about cognitive backlog in the "Simplify to engagify" chapter. By taking on too much, you run the risk of dropping the ball in other areas. In my experience, trying to do one new trick in a show is enough pressure, let alone adding two or three.

Even when your mind is entirely focused on one specific element, it's amazing how you can end up overlooking even the more basic steps. I've had instances in my own performing career when I tried to do too much and the show suffered as a result.

Keep it simple and only add one new skill, intention, or behavior to the mix at a time.

Track your results

After a trade show, a virtual training, or a keynote, I make an AAR for myself. An AAR is an After Action Report—an idea I stole from the Navy Seals. After a mission, each Seal is required to write up an AAR, recapping what happened and the lessons learned from the experience.

In my case, I document what I tried adding to the performance, how it went, and how I could improve the technique in the future. I write anything that seems relevant to the situation or that I might want to know at a later date.

Because different audiences respond differently to different types of material, I like to make notes on that type of information so I don't repeat the same mistakes in the future.

As you start to grow your skill set, track your evolution over time and make notes on how you're progressing. Review previous notes and remind yourself not only of the things you've already "learned," but where you continue to make the same mistakes. Don't get stuck—use your AARs to help you to keep growing and applying additional layers. Then use your notes to look back and see how far you've come!

Get leverage on yourself

Some of the recommendations in this book will come naturally and other parts might require considerable work and dedication. Remember the reasons you picked up this book in the first place. Remember your reasons for caring to engage. Think about the increased impact you can have and the results that can be generated from your actions. Understand the possible Return On Interactions and learn what's at stake.

Too many of us are too comfortable with the status quo. In order to drive change, we need to tap into our desire for improvement. Some of you will be motivated by new opportunities and possibilities while others find motivation in the frustration of not being noticed or listened to. Whether you're motivated towards something you want or away from what you don't want in your life, remind yourself of why you're doing the things you do.

Get the right help

As the saying goes, when the student is ready, the teacher appears. Many of the tools and skills contained in this book are quite diverse, and you may find you'll need a number of different mentors to help you reach the level of proficiency you desire. As my long-time coach, Boyd Liski, has said to me on many occasions, "There is no glory in figuring it out for yourself." Use the wisdom of others to shorten the learning curve and reap the results sooner.

Take an improv class, go to Toastmasters, or enroll in a martial arts class and get in touch with your Chi. Get a coach and then be coachable!

The world needs more of you

When I'm coaching sales teams in engagement, we use a partner exercise in which participants give a two-minute presentation to their partners and then switch roles. They then repeat the entire exercise but with one additional instruction: "Be as engaging as possible." After the second round, participants debrief, reviewing the differences between the first and second versions of the mini presentations. I'll often hear someone say, "The second time was the same, only better." The consensus is always that the second version was more engaging. My next question to the group is, "Why didn't you do that version the first time?"

The truth is, we pull punches in life to protect ourselves from standing out and being different. We don't want to take chances, for fear of failing and being rejected. In this case, some people just need permission to be more. They're fully capable but have never played full on. Maybe they were brought up to avoid being the "tallest poppy" and they have underplayed their abilities to blend into their surroundings. If everyone did that, we would be living in a sad and underperforming society.

Creating engagement requires you to be more of yourself. People find other people fascinating, especially when they're different from themselves. People can sometimes be predictable and bland—break that mold and be an original. Find your unique voice and a point of view that celebrates your differences. Give more of yourself to interactions. The world needs more people like you—people who are willing to send out their energy and individualism into the world unapologetically.

See yourself doing it

Picture your life on a timeline. A line that stretches back to the day you were born, past where you are now in the present, and stretches out into the future to the end of your life (whenever that may be). Float up above this timeline and go into the future exactly three years. In the not-so-distant future, what do you see?

Can you see yourself using the new skills you've acquired? Can you see the response you generate from those skills? How do others perceive you?

Don't just watch yourself doing it—float down into your body now and see it through your own eyes. When you see the reaction you get, how does it feel? What skills are you using? If you've followed these directions and truly see your future self thriving, then you know what skills you'll need and which you should tackle first.

Perhaps this book has opened your eyes to concepts that were unheard of to you until now. With your mind aware and focused on these ideas and the improvements you want to make, you may soon find all the necessary factors aligning in your life. Grab onto these opportunities and truly engage life!

Final thoughts

Thank you for reading this book. As you can tell, I'm passionate about creating engagement and elevating the impact of our interactions.

If you're looking to take your engagement skills to the next level, there are a number of products and services we offer at *Engagify* that might shorten that learning curve, depending on your situation.

If you make live, in-person presentations you'd receive good value out of our **Fundamental Five** presentation training. This training has been used by billion-dollar companies like Siemens and Micron to "engagify" their presenters so that even the driest technical information becomes interesting and fully resonates with the audience.

If you're someone who meets customers virtually or presents on webinars, then the **Virtual Engagement** training is the one for you. Whether you train with one of our instructors in a live virtual training, or you go it alone with the on-demand offering, this training will teach you how to get a handle on the technology, how to perform for the camera, and how to make your content more engaging.

Some people think that the old ways are the best, and you can't deny that using the phone is an oldie but a goodie. Vocal-only interactions are limited to the words you say and how you say them. If you'd like to become more expressive and learn how to harness the power of your voice, you may want to take a look at our **Vocal Engagement.** Or better yet, book an introductory call with one of our Vocal Engagement Coaches!

If you've read the whole book, then you know I've spent my share of time on trade show floors. I can tell you from experience, that booth staff who are unable or unwilling to engage are deadweight to a company looking to generate leads and make an impact. We have a number of training options to ensure your booth staff are on-point, on-process, and on fire! We can train your booth staff right before the show opens or as it approaches, in-person, or as a webinar. We can even set up each employee with an on-demand training in which they'll learn about being effective at trade shows while they wait for their flight to the show.

Everyone learns differently, so we provide several modalities. We have an online academy that allows individuals and teams of any size to train in their own time, learning from short, fast-paced videos. If you'd like a more hands-on approach, any of the trainings can also be taught through a live virtual environment and interactive coaching sessions—one-on-one or with a small team. Coaching definitely allows for the best implementation and learning.

Does your company need to be inspired to engage at a higher level? Reach out at the contact info below and inquire about our keynote presentations, designed to inspire your people to be more engaging and create unforgettable interactions.

Contact us at EngageUs@Engagify.ai to learn more about how we can engagify you, your company, or your event.

Index

www.ingramcontent.com/pod-product-compliance
Lightning Source LLC
Chambersburg PA
CBHW021924190326
41519CB00009B/904